UMFUNDISI

*"I have planted, Apollos watered,
but God has given the growth."*

(1 Cor. 3:6)

The author administers Kwambuzi's first baptism.

Umfundisi

MISSIONER TO THE ZULUS

Father Thomas M. Calkins, O.S.M.

THE BRUCE PUBLISHING COMPANY
MILWAUKEE

IMPRIMI POTEST:

LOUIS M. CORTNEY, O.S.M., *Provincial*
Province of Our Lady of Sorrows, Chicago

NIHIL OBSTAT:

THOMAS M. CALKINS, O.S.M.

NIHIL OBSTAT:

JOHN F. MURPHY, S.T.D.
Censor librorum

IMPRIMATUR:

✠ WILLIAM E. COUSINS
Archbishop of Milwaukee

July 1, 1959

Library of Congress Catalog Card Number: 59–13564

© 1959 THE BRUCE PUBLISHING COMPANY

MADE IN THE UNITED STATES OF AMERICA

TO MY FELLOW SERVITE MISSIONARIES
IN AFRICA

Foreword

A YOUNG green American missionary priest sent to South
Africa is in for it. He hits the African bush with the Gospel of
Christ, but he in turn is socked with Africa, Africans, pagan-
ism, witchcraft, and the weird customs of primitive people. It's
a new and fascinating world the moment he steps off the trans-
Atlantic plane at the airport in Johannesburg.

Timid and awkward he begins his work, stumbles along in
those huge footsteps of Apollos, watering. The seeds are here,
rich and plentiful; there's no such thing as an African atheist.
The increase will come — it's God-guaranteed. Water is all that's
needed. And while he waters, Africa avalanches herself at the
wide-eyed priest. Each day the black people and their peculiar
country bring boulders of impressions bounding on his poor
head. To cope with them in the beginning takes all he has.

After six, seven years he wakes up one morning and discovers
he's relaxed, breathing easily on his second wind. The rumbling
rush is spent. The captivating job of converting pagan natives
is becoming routine; not a dull routine — far from it — but
routine. The avalanche hasn't stopped; it never will — Africa is
in furious ferment, always new, startling, impressive — but now
the missionary feels up to things. Frankly, he's thrilled: this
watering job is no mean privilege, Apollos was no slouch.

This is the story of the little incidents that make up a modern
missionary's day in Zululand. They are tidbits of his charming
task. No mass conversions here, no hair-raising bravery with
savages. He and his fellow missionaries are not world beaters:
they are simple men with simple reactions to the strange world
of the African native.

Acknowledgment

TO OUR former Provincial, Father Srill, who, during his heartening visitation to our missions, made the remark, half suggestion, half order: "Calkins, you should write a book about this place. It's another world."

Contents

xi

Contents

ISAHLUKO 2

Ukuzalwa kuka Jesu

1 Kwathi ngalezozinsuku kwamenyezelwa isimemezelo sikaKhesare uAugustus sokuɓa kuɓalwe izwe lonke. 2 Lokhu kuɓalwa kokuqala kwenziwa nguKwirini, induna 3 yaseSiria. Ɓahamba ɓonke ɓayakuɓalwa, yilowo 4 emzini wakuɓo. Naye uJosef waphuma eGalileya, emzini waseNazaretha, wenyuka waya eJudiya emzini kaDavid, othiwa iBethlehema, ngoɓa wayengowendlu 5 nenzalo kaDavid, ukuɓa aɓalwe kanye noMaria umka-6 khe aɓemganile owayekhulelwe. Kwathi seɓekhona 7 zaphela izinsuku zokuɓa aɓelethe. Wazala inDodana yakhe yamaziɓulo, wayisonga ngezindwangu wayilalisa emkhombeni, ngokuɓa ɓaɓengenandawo endlini yezi-hambi.

Uɓikelwa aɓelusi

8 Ɓaɓekhona kulelozwe aɓelusi ɓelindile, ɓeluse umhla-9 mbi waɓo ngemilindo yoɓusuku. Nansoke ingelosi yenKosi imi ngakuɓo, nenkazimulo kaNkulunkulu iɓa-10 khanyisela, ɓesaɓa nokwesaɓa. Ingelosi yasithi kuɓo: Ningesaɓi; bekani, nginiɓikela ukuthokoza okukhulu, 11 okuzakuɓa kuɓantu ɓonke, ngoɓa emzini kaDavid niza-12 lelwe namhla umSindisi, onguKristo inKosi. Nakhu okoɓa yisiɓonakaliso kini: niyakufumana umntwana esongwe ngezindwangu, elele emkhombeni.

13 Khona masinya kwaɓa khona kanye nengelosi ama-viyo amaɓutho asezulwini eɓonga uNkulunkulu ethi:

2, 7. "InDodana yakhe yamaziɓulo". Lokhu akuqondisi ukuthi uMaria waɓa naɓanye aɓantwana, namunye, aɓaɓela-ma yona inDodana yakhe yamaziɓulo, kodwa ngendlela yo-kukhuluma kwamaJuda nomntwana owayeyedwa kunina wa-ɓizwa ngokuthi owamaziɓulo. (Beka nokwashiwo kuMt 1, 25).

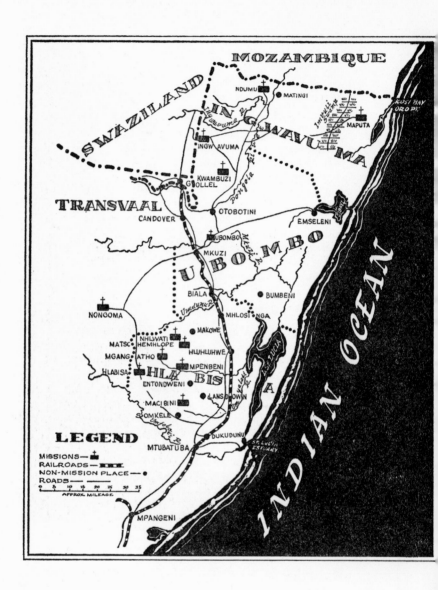

MOZAMBIQUE

SWAZILAND

INGWAVUMA

NDUMU · MATINGI

KOSI BAY
ORO PT.

MAPUTA

INGWAVUMA

KWAMBUZI
G'OLLEL

TRANSVAAL

CANDOVER

OTOBOTINI

EMSELENI

UBOMBO

MKUZI

UBOMBO

BIALA · BUMBENI

MHLOSINGA

NONGOMA

MAKOWE

NHLUVATI
MATSC HEMHLOPE
MGANG ATHO
HLABISA
ENTONDWENI
MACIBINI
S'OMKELE

HLUHLUWHE

HLABIS

MPENBENI

LANSDOWIN

A

INDIAN OCEAN

DUKUDUNU

LEGEND

MISSIONS—
RAILROADS—
NON-MISSION PLACE—●
ROADS—

0 5 10 15 20 25 30 35
APPROX. MILEAGE

MTUBATUBA

ST. LUCIA
ESTUARY

MPANGENI

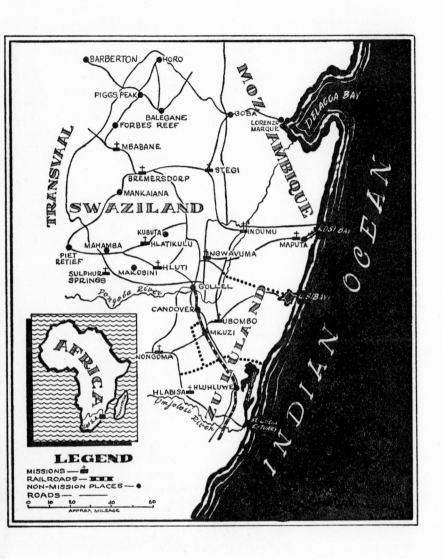

UMFUNDISI

1. "Saku Bona"

NEVER underestimate the power of a Hello. Breezy and brief or slow and prolonged, it still works wonders. In Zulu the words are easy to pronounce: "Saku bona," said slowly in a calm, soft tone. Literally they mean "I see you." Utter it today while crouching at the low entrance to some native hut in Zululand, and it's liable to bounce back at you years later with enormous results.

Sunday morning is my day to sleep at Our Lady of Ingwavuma Mission because I have the ten o'clock native Mass. On this Sunday morning, since my sermon was somewhat prepared, and the few confessions would not begin until nine, I was pounding my pillow at cruising speed as the sun rose. A sharp rap at the window bolted me awake. The native nun was on the veranda with her back to the pane; a small native boy was with her. I threw on a robe and went out.

The boy I recognized as a local herdboy who had wanted no part of our school. He came from a kraal which was not pagan, but worse, its occupants being members of a patchwork native religion known as the "Shembays." It's an impossible cult that believes God Himself is a native man living outside Durban, a large coastal city about 300 miles south of us. Send a donation to his well-oiled post box and you not only worship God, but also obtain good luck for yourself and your friends. The boy was sent to us by his father, who was dying. With about three or four Zulu words the boy delivered his message faithfully: "Go to the Roman Catholics just over the hill and

1

tell the Umfundisi I want to receive baptism before I die."
"Umfundisi" is what the Zulus call the priest. Literally it means
"one who teaches," but it is used only for those who teach things
about God, not the abc's. Ten minutes later, the sister, the boy,
and I were in the jeep bumping over the few miles to his kraal.

No doubt about the old man's dying. He was lying inside a
dingy hut, into which we crawled on our hands and knees.
His head rested on a carved wooden stump, and a dirty blanket
had been flung over him. He must have been in his eighties.
It was a chilly morning, so the three women sitting with him
had a smoky fire going in the center. The two older women
were his wives and the other his daughter. His watery, feverish
eyes closely followed the sister and me as we entered. He knew
who we were. The faces of the three women were suspicious,
but not hostile — a very important distinction when dealing with
primitive people.

The fellow wanted baptism badly. There was no going around
the subject and coming in at a gentle angle. I began this circumlocution, but the first wife cut me off by assuring me Roman
baptism was the only thing he had mumbled about during the
long night. He had a confused but sufficient idea of what it was.
I began the ceremony kneeling up straight next to the man,
but my head was in too much smoke, and my eyes got blurry.
So I bent over forward, put my elbows on the cow dung floor,
and held the ceremonial book in front of me. Good thing no
camera caught that shot. The women smiled and Sister tittered,
but I didn't mind because my head was below the low hanging
smoke line. And that portion of me in the smoke couldn't
care less.

When it was over we sat back and talked about the cool
weather, which is rare here, and the man's new name, Robert.
It was a hard one for him to pronounce — r's don't come easy
to the Zulus. I had chosen Robert after a cousin of mine. These
people have no idea of Christian names. His speech was labored,
but his thoughts were clear and coherent. Talk about facing

death properly! Here was a Catholic only a few minutes old, yet he was talking about death like a veteran Christian. He was not nervous or afraid, or dejected. He was consoled, and tried with all his fading power to grasp the simple truths we had told him about God and his soul: "You mean, Umfundisi, God loves me, has a place for me to stay with Him after I die, is going to renovate this old body, and I'll be happy forever with Him!" You could see him lurching at these new ideas as he repeated them out loud.

There was a large unanswered question in my head. The same question that pops into mind so frequently down here: why? Why does this little boy want school and eventually Catholicism, and that other does not? Why? They both know nothing about the important things, they both were asked in the same way, they both will get the same deal at school. Yet one jumps, and the other wants no part of it! Why does this third wife come to church and not the other three? Why did this old man want baptism, and further, baptism from us and not the Wesleyans or the Anglicans or any other sect around here?

He was conscious enough to be asked. And in his present state I thought if I ever get a straight answer from a native, I'll get it now. I waited for a silent moment and framed the question briefly and clearly in the best Zulu I could muster. "Why, Old Man, did you call for the Romans to baptize you and not any other church?" He could tell from the pitch of my voice and slow diction that I was not just making small talk, but was deeply interested in his answer. We stared at each other as the question passed from me and penetrated his octogenarian eyes. The three women, Sister, and I, watched him without a stir. He was thinking hard.

"I will tell you, Umfundisi, why I wanted the Roman baptism more than any other." A polite Zulu seldom bursts into a direct answer, even on his deathbed. His speech is full of flourishes and curlicues, and a question as heavy as the one I asked would have to be repeated before answering. We waited breathlessly. "I wanted Roman baptism because the Roman priest visited me." It was as simple as that. Sister and I exchanged glances, a knowing nod in her black eyes. Veteran missionary that she was she knew the inestimable power of a visit, of a Hello. I was learning it.

Our first missionaries to this area, Father Kinch and the late Father Delehanty, perhaps had visited this old man years ago. I doubt if they got much of a welcome from him or his family. The usual indifferent hello accompanied with some hollow phrases about the crops and sickness and how the monkeys are stealing everything in the fields. His wives probably did not even look up from their mat weaving. The place surely had an odor. . . . Everybody had been doubtlessly relieved when the priest made ready to leave, good-bys were profuse but empty. . . . The priest had asked for the path to the next kraal, and left at a slow pace, more tired, more discouraged, and wondering just how was he supposed to go about his immense work. Was he wasting his time and energy in this dull trudging from hut to hut ringing native doorbells?

When he died that night, Robert, for one, knew the visiting priest had not been wasting his time.

The Robert incident, however, came long after my arrival. And I don't want to get ahead of my story. I would rather take you by the hand, gently, through the amazing world of the African missionary. Tag along easily, peek over my shoulder; the sights, sounds, and experiences will be rewarding. For Africa, these lovable primitive Zulus, and the missionaries' work among them, are sure to be of interest to Americans. Theirs is an ancient, slow-moving, captivating land, forever changing, ever startling, never totally grasped.

To get at their hearts and minds you must learn the Zulu language. You hear it for the first time when the huge Constellation settles down on the runway of the sprawling Johannesburg airport. The trip from Rome has been long and tiring. The three of us are weary — Father Morgan, Brother Jack Le-May, and myself. But the mumbo jumbo of the native laborers who swarm around the plane brings you to life. You suddenly realize this is Africa. Those strong black backs handling the luggage from the underbelly of your flying monster are not Americans. Their fuzzy heads, bellowing grunts, and bare feet shout that you are now far, far away from home.

It's not easy, this native jibberish. Latin and Greek and some Hebrew were pushovers compared to it. Only recently has it been grammarized and put into writing. It laughs at logic. The vocabulary is totally different from other tongues. The root words stem from the burning soil of this dark continent, not from European civilization. It is soft and musical; a tin-eared missionary is at a terrible disadvantage; pitch and tone quality of the voice mean everything. We were laughing at the sound of it as we piled into the waiting jeep, with Father Kinch, the older missionary who had come to meet us with his Zulu manservant for the three hundred mile ride to our mission territory. It's a ride I'll never forget. Not the bouncing jeep — I had ridden in many "leaping lenas" before. Not the vast stretches of dry rolling veld of Africa's Transvaal region which we had to cross, but this grunting conversation between Father Kinch and his faithful boy, Philemon, had me spellbound. How could one ever make sense out of those strange sounds? Yet the boy and Father were carrying on smoothly, pointing out the scenery, making jokes, and perhaps talking about my own complete consternation at the newness of it all. Father Kinch, one of our first American missionaries to this part of African country, had only been here three years, but he had a firm grasp on the Zulu tongue.

After twelve grueling hours we arrived at our main mission station, Ingwavuma. That Zulu word means "roaring," named after the river that runs nearby. In 1948 our first American Servite missionaries came here and built a large priest house of cement blocks made on the site. It has eight bedrooms, a chapel, kitchen, dining room, recreation room, and is called Our Lady of Ingwavuma. Here it is where we began our Zulu lessons. A middle-aged native school teacher came to the mission and pounded away at us for six months, three hours a day, six days a week. "Mama, baba, babo, uma, ima," till we almost went mad. Vocabulary was tough enough, but the Zulu language is unique and especially difficult because of its clicking sounds. They are weird in the beginning. The letter q, for instance, if pronounced correctly sounds exactly like an American kid smacking bubblegum — I mean an expert kid who knows his business! These pops are frequent in conversation. The letter x is a real jawbreaker. You pronounce it as you would urge a horse into a gallop. The letter *c* is indescribable! You must come here for that!

There was no need to have Berlitz records to get our ears tuned to the sounds of Zulu. They were all around us at the mission; the children, sisters, cooks, workers spoke nothing else. Even without effort a newcomer is bound to pick up a few words. The best method, however, for attuning your ear is to go right out among the people in their huts. We could do this in the afternoon when the formal classes were over.

These afternoon excursions were amazing at times. In the house we spoke English, sat at tables, slept in beds, listened to the radio, while just a few minutes' walk away was a completely different civilization, centuries behind us. There people lived in grass huts, slept on mats, pounded drums, cooked with black three-legged pots over open fires, practiced witchcraft, and carried on hidden pagan rites.

Like most Americans, my idea of Africa was jungle, lions, tigers, head-hunters, and recently, Mau-Mau savages. Perhaps in other parts of Africa it's like that, but in Zululand there is very little heavy jungle and no savages. The native people do not live in clustered villages such as you see in the movies. They are spread out. One family here, another a block or two away. This gives them room for planting and cattle grazing on a small and irregular scale. This year a family will plant a meager patch of corn or potatoes or beans, next year they won't. Don't ask me why. They are like that.

An individual family lives in a small group of three or four grass huts. This the Dutch called a kraal: Gumede's kraal, Mngomezulu's kraal, to use two of the more common surnames. The headman might have three or four wives and a dozen children living there with him. Close by these huts will be his inevitable cattle kraal, a circular barnyard minus the barn where the cattle are put at night. The fence is a rough affair thrown together with heavy logs, and always in need of repair.

Between each man's kraal there might be blocks, or there might be miles and miles, of what down here we call bush. Bush is not exactly jungle. But it's not gentle forest either. It's thick, rough underbrush with low, scraggly thorn trees. Dense lush green patches are dark and damp and even frightening at first sight. This bush is the habitat of Zululand's animals. Lions have long since left, but there are plenty of small deer, various kinds of buck, baboons, rabbits, monkeys, and the ubiquitous African snakes — the python, cobra, puff adder, and worst of all, the deadly black mamba.

Small rivers and streams afford water to the parched country. They also give refuge to crocodiles. Hideous, knarled of hide, fifteen feet long, these animals lurk beneath the muddy water waiting for a stray dog or an unwary native to wander close to the hidden bank. My first trip to the hospital was with a native woman whose thigh had been torn by the snapping jaws of a croc as she washed in a stream. She was lucky not to have been belted into the water by his swift strong tail. Hippos, too, stroll up and down the streams, submerging to their eyes and nostrils in daylight and coming out to feed at night. And then, there is the "old man" himself, Mr. Elephant, who also likes to stay close to the rivers. In spite of his bulk, he's seldom seen because he hides in the heaviest bush and is always on the move avoiding man. But there is no doubt of his presence when you find an uprooted tree across the road, or a ravaged field, or his gigantic leavings.

In the beginning it's better to go alone to visit the natives in the bush, without even a native boy, because in that way you must speak Zulu. Even after months in Zulu class all you are sure of is "hello," "good-by," and "oh." The first time I sprung my hello on an unsuspecting native, he just stared blankly at me and tightened his grip on the bushknife he was carrying. Another time I saw a pleasant looking fellow and labored over my greeting to him; he smiled calmly and answered in perfect English, "I'm fine, Father, how are you?" He was a native teacher.

The bush is laced with footpaths and it's not good to wander off these. While walking along one of these paths in the afternoon a few months after I had arrived in Ingwavuma, I noticed an old fellow sitting in front of a well-built hut. The Zulus are a very sociable tribe and are pleased with visitors, even those with little knowledge of Zulu. This fellow answered my wave eagerly, so I sauntered over primed with a practiced "hello, and how are you?" I blurted it out to him then stood and looked simple — not a hard thing for me to do.

He had a friendly manner and invited me to sit on the rock next to him. I managed to get a few ideas over: I was a new Roman priest, just learning Zulu (he would never guess!) and I liked his beautiful country. He listened politely but preferred to talk himself, whether I understood or not. It seems he was telling me about his days in the South African Native Army. His machine-gun Zulu was impossible to catch but his gestures kept me on the track. Suddenly in the midst of his swift Zulu came these words in English: "Come on you bloody fools!" Really! Evidently he was repeating one of his officer's remarks. He saw I liked it; in fact, I nearly split, so he kept repeating it. His four wives, hearing the commotion, put their heads out of the hut, and he blasted at them with it too!

During my visit there his many children were running around the yard playing with dogs and chickens, and sneaking quick looks at the white man talking to papa. Another woman happened by and my talkative pal told her I was a priest. She gave me a respectful greeting, then unleashed her tongue on the old guy, telling him he should listen to what I say, and stop drinking native beer, and not be so lazy, and go to church — on and on unmercifully. The fellow humbly put his head down and looked thoroughly beaten. At the peak of Miss Righteousness' tirade he slyly looked over at me, caught my eye and winked. I thought of Micawber and W. C. Fields. These natives may not be so different from us after all.

Soon I pointed to my watch and motioned that I must be going. He looked at the sun and nodded. He called his wives and children around to say good-by, then grunted an order which sent about five little kids chasing a choice chicken around the yard. The new priest was to get a gift. They brought it to papa and he handed it to me. I clumsily took it, and not being used to handling live chickens, I let it get away. He recovered it, tied its legs, then tucked it under his arm showing me how to carry it. As he did this he strutted across the yard in perfect imitation of my barrelly walk. Natives are excellent mimics. He had watched me coming over the hill toward his kraal and had my walk down exactly. I took the chicken, thanked him warmly, then waltzed out of the yard exaggerating my rolling gait. Bob Hope never got a better laugh.

As I went home, back to the twentieth century a few miles away, I wondered if the old fellow will always be so friendly toward me. Will he like it when my Zulu gets better and someday, after listening to one of his army stories, I confidentially nudge him in the side with: "That's a good one all right, you got a million of 'em. But, by the way, Doc, you know those wives you got over there? They're really only your concubines; and all these children around here — nothing but a lot of naked little you-know-whats!"

2. The Pay-Off

ZULU lessons were soon over. The six months went quickly, and — frankly — quite miserably. But there was enough Zulu in my head to enable me to hear confessions and deliver a hesitating sermon. It was time to be assigned to one of the missions in the vast virgin area given over to the American Province of Servite Fathers by the Propagation of the Faith in Rome. The Pope was counting on us, the natives needed us, why wait?

Our mission territory is located in the northeast corner of the Union of South Africa in the Province of Natal. Portuguese East Africa, or Mozambique, borders us on the north; the Indian Ocean laps us on the east. Roughly estimated, the area extends about one hundred and fifty miles north and south and about sixty miles east and west. That's a man-size chunk of hinterland! The native population of this chunk is about one hundred and seventy-five thousand; the whites number close to a thousand. Most of it is low veld — that is, flatlands — and bush, not much above sea level; but there is a mountain range running north and south dividing the area. This strip of mountains, about two thousand feet high, called the Ubombo Range, continues in an unbroken line all the way up to Egypt.

In the northeast corner of this territory we have a mission aptly called Star of the Sea. It is located three miles inland from the shore of the Indian Ocean, and seven miles south of the Mozambique border. It was to this mission I was sent for my first assignment.

The day was memorable. I packed my Zulu books and few

belongings into the jeep and drove east to the Pongola River. After some trouble getting my overloaded jeep onto the broken-down pont used to cross the river, I drove up the other bank and across thirty-five miles of sand country. There was no need to steer the jeep. I just put it in four-wheel drive, second gear, and let it grind itself along in the bumpy twin ruts. The wheels would not veer off the tracks even if you turned them.

Star of the Sea was well prepared for its first assistant priest. Father Delehanty, the pastor there, was one of the original pioneers who had come to South Africa with Father Kinch in 1948. He was a big, noisy Irishman whom I had known for years in Chicago and I was happy to be assigned as his assistant. With him at Star of the Sea was Brother Tim Culhane, a former teacher at St. Philip's High School in Chicago and an old friend of our family. It promised to be a nice setup in this forsaken bush, where close friends are important. They welcomed me with the red-carpet treatment. I recall their rushing out to meet the jeep and helping me with my luggage. The all-day trip had been tiring and before we knew it, each had a fat glass with ice cubes clinking in good Irish whiskey. There was a homemade sign pinned on my bedroom door: "Welcome, Punchy, to Star of the Sea." I felt at home.

In the morning they took me around the mission. At that time there were only two main buildings up, the school and the priests' house. Both were small but adequate, built by Tim out of cement blocks which he had made on the site. Electricity came from a balky home generating plant, and water was pumped by an equally temperamental engine from a nearby stream. There were a few boy and girl boarders from faraway areas living at the mission. They slept in the school with the teacher. The terrain was much different from that of Ingwavuma. Here we were in flat sand country, whereas Ingwavuma was on top of a fertile mountain. The tribe here was the Thongas, a more backward and simple group than the Zulus of Ingwavuma. Their language was slightly different, though they could understand and speak the more common Zulu. Our main job, as Father Delehanty explained to me that first morning, was to recruit kids for the school. There were only thirty-five now and we had room for over a hundred.

It was bewildering, this new work. The strange language, the hot sun, the rough sand country, the native people. I was in their midst now, trying to know them, aching to lead them. Every day was different, new, startling. One was spent bandaging their sores, another hauling supplies, then another back at the Zulu book for new words and ways to put them together.

During the week much of the missionary's work is only remotely religious. He directs native laborers, chats for hours listening to their woes, and spends much of his time just getting to places by foot, by horse, and by jeep. Sunday, however, is pay-off day. That may be an undignified name but it is a very accurate one for God's Day on the missions. It's the time for gauging progress, Sunday morning. It's the day when people give back; the day on which their turn comes to respond to grace and all the secondary means you have been using on them during the week. While visiting the huts the people might treat you as a king; when they come around for medicine and favors they could not be more respectful. But this means little in the long run if they don't attend church on Sunday. Because there we get our heavy blows in, the Mass, catechism, sermon, benediction. There, in church, is our golden opportunity to pass on all this Good News we have for them.

The parish scene around our place on Sunday is far different from that at home. Only the Mass is the same. At Star of the Sea Mission, the people congregate around the kitchen waiting for the priest to emerge. Native women mostly, squatting in sweaty, dirty, oily old skirts, a crying baby strapped on their backs. What do they want? It could be anything — a few ears of corn, some sugar, a headache pill. If there's a rag around their mouths you know they have a tooth to be pulled; you've been instructed a bit about this before coming over. The dental forceps are handy, so you dig in. No anesthetic, just a good grip on the tooth, a strong hold on the jaw, a few firm tugs, low painful moans, a final twist, and out it comes. Not the most liturgical preparation for the celebration of Mass!

Our arrangement for saying Mass was typical for a budding mission. The schoolroom was used as a church. On the teacher's desk in front we set up the portable altar. The native teacher decorated it with local flowers and palm branches. When done up well it gave the people the idea that the classroom had suddenly become a place of reverence and solemnity. In the beginning we had only one Mass on Sunday, Father Delehanty and I taking turns.

By ten o'clock, if the weather is good and the local native beer is bad, the place is crowded. By ten fifteen the room is crawling with natives. They're in the aisle, on the desks, in the seats, up front close around the altar. At any time during the Mass I can reach out and tap four or five, they're so close. One Sunday I was stumbling through St. Paul's Epistle, something about kicking against the goad, when suddenly the book, stand, and all were knocked from in front of me. Two kids, standing next to the altar, had got in a scrap and accidentally hit the bookstand. I in turn accidentally planted my foot on their shins as I picked up the debris.

In a way our Sunday Mass is a liturgist's nightmare. By that I mean, things don't always go according to the rules. During the Mass anything can happen back there in the congregation. It must be remembered that these people are raw pagans right out of the bush — perhaps not one baptized Catholic among them. They vaguely know what a church is for, have no idea of the Mass. Women nurse babies, men take snuff, kids play games. They wander in and out freely. Some are necessary exits for the kids and babies; often these necessary exits are too late — but no one bats an eye.

The sermon is a trying time for both priest and congregation. The first time I preached at Star of the Sea I had them spellbound, in dead silence. The reason was that I had a new face and a new language. My nervous sputtering of mumbo-jumbo Zulu had them dumfounded. I called a little boy over afterward, a pal of mine, and asked him if he had understood what I preached. He thought for a minute, looked at me despairingly and said: "Ai khona, Umfundisi, luto." Which means, "No, Father, not a darn thing."

The part of Sunday morning that the natives like best is the gossip period after Mass. Gregarious by nature, they welcome getting together on Sunday. They mill around in front for an hour, talking about everything. And Father must listen to the aches and pains of the elderly people, laugh at jokes he doesn't understand, crack a few corny ones himself, and try not to miss a face or greeting.

This latter is important, as I found out. Visiting a hut one day a woman promised me she would come to church next Sunday; she lived deep in the bush and dressed like it, cattle skin skirt, some beads on her ankles, and that was all. A month later I went back to her and asked why she didn't keep her promise. She said she came all right, but since I didn't greet her she did not come back. The fact was I didn't recognize her. When she came to church she had a clean face and an old house dress on, and it was too big a change for me from her bush clothing.

Clothing of the natives is not the important item in Catholic missionaries' eyes that it is among the non-Catholics. We teach them modesty, of course, but modesty and scant clothing are not incompatible for the Zulu. It's best to leave it up to themselves for the most part. Some come to church in their native dress, and we welcome them. For the men, that's an animal loinskin tied with leather thongs. For the women, it's a cowhide skirt with a piece of material thrown over the shoulders loosely. Often this material is just carried, not worn. The majority, however, who attend church manage to rustle up some kind of white-people's clothing, an old shirt and pants for the men, and a battered dress of some sort for the women.

Each regular churchgoer gets a catechism card which the priest signs during this after-Mass gossip period. At that time there were about thirty-five card holders. It's a good check on the people, and gives us a chance to say a few words to each one. When they miss we put an x in that Sunday's square. We make a big fuss over these x's so that they dislike getting them. And if their card has too many x's they don't get a Sacred Heart Badge pinned on them; this is another great evil in their eyes. With some of the more undressed, even when they deserve the badge, it's a problem finding a place to pin it without drawing blood. In that case we just give them the badge and tell them to hang it on a string around their neck.

When finished, you leave the schoolroom church and go back to the priests' house for coffee, and there again you find a small group of natives waiting. This is the inner circle of the parish. They've been coming a long time and consider it beneath themselves to petition you in front of the ordinary peasants. There may be seven or eight of them, women mostly — the first ones who became interested in your work. Others perhaps laughed at them when they returned every Sunday to hear more about this Man called Christ; but they didn't mind — something told them the missionaries weren't out here for nothing. They became familiar with the priests, could laugh with them, respected them, felt at home with them even when on mission grounds. One old toothless woman who was the only prospect present on the first Sunday when Father Delahanty celebrated Mass, has never returned to the schoolroom for Mass, but comes to the mission every Sunday. She takes it upon herself to chase the others into the schoolroom, but she claims, since she was the first, she needs no more religion: she's all filled up. She and the others corner you here. Their wants are the same: a few aspirins; a clean bandage on an old sore; something for a pain in the stomach, for the baby with worms; a half crown till next month.

It's past noon when you get to your coffee.

Back they go to their kraals, those handfuls of ignorant, faithful churchgoers. They are the first in this Star of the Sea area to become interested in truths that count. You watch them disappear slowly over the gently rolling hills, laughing and talking along the narrow twisting paths until you can hear them and see them no longer. From the mound on which the mission is built your eyes lift and leap out for forty miles over hot, African low veld. That's the parish out there. It doesn't look like much: low stunted trees, blazing patches of sand in the hot sun, thick bush country. But that bush is teeming with natives. Natives who know nothing about you or the wonders you have for them. It's fine to have Sunday pay-offs for the sixty or seventy who have just left, but the problem is how to get at those thousands, tens of thousands, down there in the bush.

One of the means used to get in touch with these outlying districts is the kraal Mass. We choose a new area and have a talk with the catechist. He's a missionary priest's right arm, the catechist. Usually a middle-aged native trained well in the truths of Catholicism, he's employed by the priest to act as liaison man between the white priest and the black people. He knows their ways, their language, and their thoughts as the priest could never know. With simple orders he's sent to the proposed new district: tell the people a priest is coming, and select a decent hut for Mass.

Not many months after my arrival at Star of the Sea, with the approval of Father Delahanty, I sent the catechist to a particular area some thirty miles from the Mission. He came back with the news: "All the people there are glad you want to come, Father, but they would not offer their huts for Mass." That's native diplomacy for "Stay out!" I sent him back with the message: "Since you people are so glad Father wants to visit you, and since there are so many of you, Father will say Mass for you under a tree." The catechist then selected a tree and told the natives my exact date, which was to be on a weekday morning about a week after his visit.

That "breaking in" day had to be planned well, for it's important. First impressions are everything to natives, and this will be their first view of a priest, Mass, Catholicism. I had the Mass kit cleaned well: shining candlesticks and snow-white altar linen might impress these pagans as words and persuasion might never do. There were some native girl school children boarding at the mission whom we had trained to sing parts of the Mass. From these I selected three to make up our choir at the kraal Mass; not the foghorns who irk me on Monday mornings, and not the pip-squeaks who can't be heard, but three full-throated lasses — who sang all the way there and back just to show me what a good choice I had made.

Early on a pleasant weekday morning, the catechist, choir girls, and I piled into the jeep and started out. Our hopes were high for a successful breakthrough in that hot heathen veld. After two hours of bouncing through bush we arrived at the appointed tree. It alone was there waiting. I gave the catechist a look, but he nervously assured me some would show, a handful anyhow. Natives have no Elgins, so the time of Mass had been indicated by pointing to where the sun would be at about ten o'clock. The catechist looked up and said we were early.

The first customer for our debut was a little girl of about ten carrying a small homemade table on her head. She did not have one stitch of clothes on, not even the woven wristband the most shameless wear. The table was for the Umfundisi, as the catechist had asked. It was far too rickety for Mass, but I thanked her for it, patted her tufted head, and told her to run home and tell her mommy and daddy to come. She said a few of her mommies were on the way, but the others wanted to stay home with daddy. Two curious herdboys wandered by eyeing me and their goats: I nailed them down with a piece of candy. Anything for numbers this first time.

Since I could not use the table for Mass, I set up the portable altar on the tail gate of the jeep. We hacked down bushes and drove the front of the jeep into the opening; this gave room for me and the congregation under the shade of the tree. The sun was beginning to get nasty. The altar was at a rakish angle — missal, candlesticks, chalice tended to slide off to the right. I employed the two small herdboys, who had dreadful b.o., to hold the candlesticks, and little Lady Godiva was to keep the book in place and hold the pages from blowing. They were thrilled to put their dirty hands on anything. I would keep a wary eye on the chalice and hope for the best.

In such a remote area we could not expect many people. Ten would be good, five not disappointing. Fifteen, and I call the bishop for a confirmation date! Today I had about eight adults and five kids; babies don't count, there's one on every woman's back, effortlessly strapped there with cowhide. The catechist arranged the people so they squatted comfortably on the sand behind me. I vested slowly knowing that all the black eyes were not missing a thing. Over my short pants and T-shirt went the heavy black Servite religious habit, and over that the Mass vestments. The strange clothes had the natives spellbound. Before Mass I said hardly a word to the people — I was too cranky from the fast. After Mass and coffee I would be a new man, all set for smiles and gab.

To appreciate it, you have to be there when a group of backwoods natives witness Mass for the first time. No matter how often I celebrate in different virgin areas it's always a new experience. Their sharp eyes miss nothing; they catch the hundred minute movements of the priest. Their expressive faces show what's in their minds — usually utter bewilderment. When I swing around for the *Dominus Vobiscum* I scan them. The rules tell the priest to keep his eyes down for this, but the Pope himself might look up if he were in my shoes at these kraal Masses.

The good people wonder just what I will do next. "Lookit," they whisper, "he's kissing that thing. And the way he bends over, ough!" Some are agape, even dribbling at the chin, for the whole Mass. Others get weary from continuous consternation.

Everybody perks when the priest genuflects. "Imagine a white man doing that! That! What's the bell ringing for? Lookit the way he lifts up that round white thing away over his head . . . And then the shiny cup! Why are the singing girls and catechist so quiet now, and they're kneeling so straight? What is this business?"

In the sermon you try to tell them something about "this business." But it's baffling to you as well; how can you explain it to them! You go to something more general than the Mass: Christ and the Church. That's no good either. To them Christ is just a name, and Church is a total blank. God is your oasis. Him they know. Him they talk about, *Unkulunkhulu*, the Great Great One. So you give them some ideas about God. They have a few distorted ones themselves; don't dare disturb those too suddenly. Later you may be able to dislodge them, ever so gently. For now just slip in some true notions of God; then tell them how happy you are to be there and what a terribly hot day it is and how their corn is burnt and how sick they are with malaria and how water is scarce, etc.

When you finish the sermon you say to yourself, now all I have to do is celebrate Mass. But that's not easy. The distractions for the priest at such a Mass are maddening. Something is always falling off the portable altar. The candles don't burn correctly. Gentle winds raise havoc with the Host and missal pages. And this morning there were the two fragrant little boys and an unblushing sun worshiper holding down the altar cloths, the missal pages, the chalice veil.

These three kids, helpful as they were, were also all over my back. I could not move a foot without first moving one of them. The undraped and unabashed little girl took a liking to me, and while dutifully holding the missal pages, also affectionately sidled up to me throughout the Mass. *Sursum Corda* (Lift up your hearts). You answer yourself, *Habemus ad Dominum* (We have — to God). The familiar Latin rolls off easily enough. But you don't lift up your heart at all because the little boy holding the candlestick with one hand is violently picking his flat dirty nose with the other! Christ saw all this coming, you know that. And He agreed. So you stumble on and bring Him there, onto the tail gate of the jeep under the thorn-apple tree.

It's a relief to take off the hot vestments. The sweat didn't reach through to the alb and chasuble, but the other clothes are soaked. When the people see the catechist putting things away they loosen up and the atmosphere becomes less tense. In a few minutes they are talking in their usual way. I had noticed them staring at the crucifix. Before putting it in the kit I brought it near them and asked what they thought it was. The close view made them draw breath in awe. A little old lady squinting hard at it was the first to hazard an answer: "It's a baboon hung up to dry." The others did not disagree.

You can see how badly they are in need of us, of the Mass. They don't understand, of course, the stupendous mystery that just took place; they may even laugh and ridicule it later. But the priest knows the awful power of the Mass, especially in spiritually barren areas where it has never been celebrated, where Christ has never been brought, and where He surely wants to be. If the missionary priest had to depend solely on himself and not on his tremendous powers of celebrating Mass, he would never dare attempt this mammoth job. How could he? He's no match for paganism, witchcraft, perhaps even the devil himself! The Mass is a match, a sure Thing.

Immediately after Mass I go to my thermos bottle for coffee and a sandwich, and with these I make my thanksgiving. Grateful for the food, and a thousand times more grateful for this mission work, I can't think of any other padre in the whole world I'd change places with!

Because of my white skin I am left quite alone while eating — and it's not unpleasant. For one thing, I get a chance to relax and gather some thoughts about this new area. Missionaries are in the watering business, like Apollos. In each field we must figure out the best means for this watering: a clinic, a school?

A movie occasionally with religious plugs between reels? The latter feels Protestant but it could have results. . . . Or just coast along with these outdoor Masses once a month until a few catechumens pop their heads out of the bush? . . . Hummm, this bread tastes good, and I hope the boss isn't thinking of sending me back home.

On another occasion when the catechist and I were out looking for a place to say Mass in a distant area, we came upon a large kraal with its group of huts surrounding a yard. The people in the yard stopped and stared as we passed them on our way to the headman. What could we possibly want — a young whiteman in short pants, funny looking collar, white sun helmet, and a tall native with a commanding look? The whiteman did not carry a revolver, so he wasn't a policeman; nor was his native servant carrying a rifle, so he wasn't a hunter. The headman eyed me steadily, boldly; it was not the look of a friendly man.

With such a native, greeting etiquette is quickly finished and my catechist came to the point. He spoke up in a gentle, dignified tone (tones are extremely important in Zulu). "This white man is a Roman Catholic priest and I am his catechist, and we are looking for a kraal to worship God. We request yours." Not a feature moved on the headman's large strong face. His muscular, half-naked body remained rigid. The silence was tense. His wives put their eyes down, the children hardly breathed. His shifty glance shot from the catechist to me and the beady pig eyes set close together were defiant. I met his cold stare, looked at it and through it with some ice of my own: for me to give an inch by looking away or showing timidity would not do. His simple mind would interpret that as weakness in me and everything I stood for. From deep in his barrel chest three Zulu words rumbled out, "No, I refuse."

The catechist was quiet. Being a native, he knew the answer was final. I didn't, and began to reason with him in well-prac- ticed Zulu. "But there is no church in this area, and we want to give you and your people an opportunity to worship God. You yourself know well that all people must worship God regularly, you know that — " He cut me off. "Tell your priest," he said, speaking to the catechist — his tone was respectful enough, I'm white and this is South Africa, but it had a ring of finality — "Tell your priest, catechist, that I am finished with the question." The catechist knew I caught his Zulu and remained silent. I was silent, too, for a long moment. Then I put my hand out to him and each of his wives, and we left.

It's a country of obstacles, South Africa, for the Catholic missionary especially. They come at him daily in all sizes and from all angles, many unpredictable, many insurmountable — all difficult. The natives are ignorant and suspicious, the whites can be unfriendly, and the country itself is hot and hard. Alligator skin would be the proper equipment for weathering such a refusal as we got from that headman, but it's not standard on missionaries in the low-price field. A cut like that can go deep. In the beginning you come away reeling: "Don't these people know a good thing when they see it! Why not worship God! What've they got to lose!" After a while you develop calluses. Besides, foreign missionaries are not usually made of tender timber. God's grace gives them shoulder pads to handle the occasional rough and tumble of the bush.

We shook off the sting of the headman's rebuff. We searched some more and came upon a second large kraal. The name of the headman here was Mashaba, a totally different man from the first. In a calm, manly way he was deeply delighted to have "men of God" (his colorful Zulu for the catechist and me) visit his home. He set out his best grass mats in his cleanly swept sleeping hut. When he was sure we were comfortable, and I was with my back against the mud wall and my tanned bow legs stretched out, he quietly came around to the purpose of our visit. Before asking, we could see he was more than willing. The catechist put the question: "Would you mind if the priest held services in your kraal?" The man didn't beam or jump with joy, he seemed more deeply moved than that. He just answered slowly, "Can a man refuse messengers from the Great Great One?"

In three months poor Mashaba would be receiving messengers sent by another great one, but not ours. The Mass date was arranged in a few minutes. We would come next Saturday and on every first Saturday of the month thereafter. It worked in fine with my schedule. I looked at the hut — that box in the corner would do for a table, the dark hut would be all right for reading the missal when the candles were lit, and it was large enough to hold the few we would get.

He was not completely ignorant of Christian worship, our host Mashaba. I saw that on the very next visit, the following first Saturday of the month. Somewhere along the line he must have attended prayer meetings of rare vintage. As I began the prayers of Mass I could hear from behind me a low "Aye-yea-men," said with great emotion. By the time I got to the Gospel, he had gone through his whole repertoire of theology, "Alleluja, oh Jehovah. I'm a sinner. Let's live it up!" It wasn't raining inside Mashaba!

After Mass, Mashaba offered another surprise in his bungling well-intentioned way. While I was putting the vestments back into the kit, he stood up and called for everyone's attention. I too paused. He grandly motioned me to a stool while he poised himself in front of us. What's coming now? I thought. Formally, and sincerely, too, he thanked me for coming, paid high compliments all around, and to my great surprise quoted — in Zulu of course — a text I had just read from the Gospel and had preached on, about Christ being the Good Shepherd. It's good with the natives and I use it constantly. Then he completely non-plused me, this resourceful Mashaba, by tearing into a very heated rehash of my sermon! He was cutting in on the act!

I'm a patient man with these likable natives, but a good humble preaching-man Servite wants no guy horning in, not even a goodhearted Mashaba! So I gave my catechist the eye — he

was just as surprised as I — and smoothly he got up and
slowed down Mashaba's revved-up motor. The flywheel was
just about off. In a few soft-spoken words the catechist let
Mashaba know that Father is the only one who does the preaching in the Roman Church. Catholics can get up and talk about
anything under the sun, but when it comes to doctrine or morals,
they listen. Priests study many long years for just that purpose.
The catechist was gentle and delicate, and Mashaba was not hurt
at all. He seemed to realize humbly how much he had yet to
learn about proper worship of God.

But that time will never come for Mashaba. Two more first
Saturdays I visited his kraal and had Mass. It was one of the
most promising kraal-Mass outstations. Mashaba himself was
leading the pack, struggling over the Hail Mary, Apostles' Creed,
and three Persons in One God. But the third time I arrived
Mashaba was not there. Instead I found a fresh mound of dirt
in the center of the yard; it was carefully covered with rocks,
selected and arranged in oblong shape. His two wives had black
cloth draped over their hips.

About a week before, Mashaba had gone off to the river to
wash himself. He didn't return that night, so the next day his
wives and others looked for him. They found his footprints in
the sand. The tracks went into the river, out again, and into the
thick underbrush that lines the large Usutu River. There were
no tracks coming out of the bush, and no trace of him in the
bush. They reported his disappearance to the police.

The South African police have a large job on their hands.
They are white, as are all the civil authorities here, yet most of
their work is with blacks. They have had much experience in
dealing with natives, and many of them can speak Zulu like a
native; still that difference of skin puts them worlds away.
Hence, when a case arises like that of the disappearance of
Mashaba, they are often at a loss, even though they do have
native constables to assist them, constables who carry clubs, not
firearms.

Days after Mashaba was reported missing, the police managed to get the whole story from an eyewitness who had seen the three men who killed Mashaba. The story is gruesome because it was a "ritual murder." In spite of the vigorous fight by church bodies and the government against this diabolical practice, ritual murder is far from rare. It might happen two or three times a year in the same locality.

For ritual murder a victim is selected in some occult manner. He or she may be of another tribe or the same tribe, old or young. The person is taken by surprise, and while he is still alive various portions of the victim's body are cut out by a witch doctor; then he is left to die. The removed portions of flesh are dried out, ground into fine powder, and worked over with ancient rites. This powder is considered as "strong medicine," used perhaps to cure the sickness of a chief, to help a sterile woman, to give a good crop, to curse an enemy.

Mashaba's death was seen by this eyewitness who happened to be fishing in a hidden place on the opposite side of the river. Mashaba came out of the river after washing, went into the bush and was attacked with clubs and knives by the three men. Later the witness saw the three men push what remained of him into the Usutu River and force it out to the middle where the water is fast flowing. They had hacked off his head and arms, and had taken out his heart. The hole in Mashaba's yard was a grave for his belongings only, none of his body was recovered. Before they were taken, the three murderers had already passed on the medicine to other witch doctors whose names they would never reveal.

At Mass that day the sermon was a natural. I told them of Baptism of Desire and its rich rewards. They learned how a person, like Mashaba, when enlightened about God's way of entering heaven through baptism, can get there by desiring to start on the way though never actually receiving the water on his head. God is no quibbler. He wanted Mashaba, and Mashaba in his way wanted God. They listened closely, breathlessly.

3. Outstations

IN THE encyclical of Pope Benedict XV, *Maximum Illud,* on the foreign missions, the Holy Father advises us to spread out. "The first care of one who is at the head of a mission is to extend the work and bring it to completion. For as the whole country which lies within the limits of his mission is entrusted to his care, he must seek to work out the salvation of all those who inhabit that country. Hence when he has converted a few thousand out of an extensive population, he should not draw the line there and rest contented. He must, no doubt, foster, bring up and protect those whom Jesus Christ has begotten, nor should he allow them to drift and perish. But let him not imagine that he has done his duty, unless he strives with all his strength and without flagging to bring Christian truth and life within the reach of all the others, whose number is infinitely greater" (Para. 7).

It's of the very essence of our task here to increase. We are not pastors in the strict sense, but missionaries. Pastors will come after us. Our job is to plant the Church, here, there, and every-where. To be content and satisfied with present progress is not for the missionary; for him that's a disease. When he has a seedling, a Catholicism growing healthy and strong in one area, he must employ one hand to maintain that and keep it coming, and use the other to scratch around in new areas. For this we need outstations. Outstations are the backbone of the future Church here. And outstations in this country, believe me, are not easy to get.

The territory assigned to us, not Star of the Sea parish alone, contains four different categories of land. First, there are the European Townships, small centers two or three miles square cut up into one-acre plots, and declared by law to be for European residents only; second, European Farmlands, huge tracts of land owned and farmed by white people with many native laborers living and working on them; third, there are the Crown Lands, large areas retained by the government for whatever use it may want. Great numbers of natives live on these lands, since the government has not yet determined what it intends to do with them. Finally, there are the Native Reserves, the proper home and land of the natives, where the majority of natives live.

To obtain a piece of land in the European Township you need money and luck. The acreage is there, often not being used, but perhaps it's not up for sale, or is for sale for an absurdly high price. Farmlands can be bought, and reasonably, but missionaries are not supposed to be farmers. Crown Lands are out — the government won't let you even think about a plot in them. The Native Reserves provide the best opportunity although much red tape needs to be cut before it is possible to get a site there.

For such a worthy cause as a native primary school backed with the finances of Catholic American dollars you would think that one or two acres on this vast continent could be had for the asking. But, everybody is in the ball game — in it and against the Catholic missionary. The natives: "We like our paganism, our many wives, our ageless ways — don't bother us with book learning and prayers and all that rubbish about Jesus Christ." The government: "You missionaries often spoil the natives terribly; then they bother us. Why not leave them alone; let us handle them our way?" The Protestants (not all — many of the Protestant missionaries we have met here are our good friends, and often outdo us in zeal; but that squint-eyed, dramatically heroic, narrow-lipped, intense missionary type): "My dear brethren, the Catholics are trying to get into your territory to lead you to perdition and to make you adore a woman called Mary. The priests not only have horns but they don't have wives; hence keep an eye on your girls."

After one year, Star of the Sea Mission lost its assistant priest. I was transferred to the southern end of our territory, about one hundred and twenty miles away, and given charge of our Good Shepherd Mission. It was not easy to leave Star of the Sea's good people. In that short, fast-moving year we had grown fond of each other. My Zulu had become more fluent and it was a genuine thrill to make them laugh during the catechism classes, and occasionally during a sermon. I got to know many first names, and they dubbed me with a few of their own. Natives give their own special Zulu names to the handful of white people living in their area. Besides the usual Umfundisi, which they call every minister of religion, I had the less dignified "Mvana Omcane" (pronounced as I have spelled it), which means "little lamb." I'm small in stature and I suppose the initial shyness I had in first visiting their huts gave them the idea of lamb. Yes, they also called me "Mvooboo," which means hippo. But that is a story for a later chapter.

Good Shepherd Mission was a great change from Star of the Sea. The terrain is mountainous — in fact, it's located on the same mountain range as Ingwavuma Mission is, the Ubombo Range, about eighty miles farther south as the crow flies, but about one hundred and twenty miles by road — not flat sand lands as is Star of the Sea. The Mission was not started by our American Servites but by German Benedictines in 1932. Many of the Catholics in the area are second generation Christians, and that makes a great difference; children of Catholic parents are worlds apart in religious outlook from children of pagan parents. The people are pure Zulu stock, no mixtures with the Thonga Tribe, as in Star of the Sea. Good Shepherd is in the heart of Zululand, the Paramount King of the Zulus, Cyprian Dinizulu, lives only about twenty miles away. Their language is classic Zulu and they are proud of it. The natives seemed cleaner, more attractive, more cultured than any I had known.

At the time of my arrival the Mission was not called by the English name Good Shepherd; the Zulu words meaning good shepherd were used as the title, "Umalusi Omuhle," pronounced as it is spelled, with the exception of that *hl* in the second word, meaning good. The *hl* is sounded with a slushing of the tongue. Though Good Shepherd Mission was founded in 1932, it was only an outstation until we American Servites took it over in April of 1951. Our first resident Servite there was Father Hayden, who returned to America for reasons of health.

Because it was only an outstation for so many years it was not much to look at physically. There was a small two-room school building made of cement blocks. The school had about thirty children in it. A few hundred yards from the school was another small cement block building of four rooms, our home. Brother John Bardini, the Servite lay brother assigned to Good Shepherd with me, originally from Siena, Italy, slept in one room, I in another. The third was a visitor's room, and the fourth we used as our chapel. It was highly inadequate. Our kitchen and dining room were a small wooden shack behind the bedrooms.

It took me a few months to get used to the change. However, here, as in every mission, the idea was to advance, spread out, increase. Missionaries are never at a loss for knowing what the prime object is in their work. It's simply: spread out. Take care of what you've already acquired in souls, don't spread too thin, but never be satisfied with the "status quo." Outstations are the answer to this spread out idea. Here, there, and everywhere is fine for them. One or two acres of land is sufficient to lay the seed for a whole new parish. It may take fifty or a hundred years to grow, but the seed can be planted anytime, and should be sown immediately.

Outstations were in my thoughts day and night at Good Shepherd Mission. But they are not to be had by mere dreaming.

There are reams of red tape to get through. You need the local natives' and their chief's consent to acquire the land. They must have many meetings and powwows for this, which might go on for a year. And, although the natives' consent is necessary beforehand, the government itself has the final word on whether the mission gets the outstation site. In other words, acquiring outstations is somewhat of a hit-or-miss affair. You get them by alertness, by keeping roving eyes open, ever at the ready to leap into a new opportunity. Even the most discouraging lead might eventually pay off. After all, we're not alone on this job; He's up there running the whole show.

After I had been at Good Shepherd a few months I set off to follow a hunch given me by a Catholic native about obtaining an outstation site in a forgotten area about twenty miles from the mission. I had visited the area previously and had often thought how nearly ideal it would be for an outstation. One acre of land there, and we would be in business. My catechist, Thomas, and I first went to the local subchief of the proposed spot. Nduna is the Zulu name for these subchiefs. They are often more difficult to deal with than the chief himself, but you dare not bypass them. Thomas thought it better I stay in the car while he went and talked. In ten minutes he and the Nduna came out agreeing. So far so good. The three of us drove off to see the chief of the Zulus of that area, the fabulously rich Mtubatuba. He died recently, but at that time he was the most powerful chief under the Zulu King Cyprian Dinizulu. This visit deserves space.

A good criterion for judging a native's wealth and standing in the tribe is the size of his cattle kraal, also the number of huts in his group. We could see Mtubatuba's place for miles before we reached it. His cattle kraal was something like a square city block, and full — by far the greatest display of native wealth I had ever seen. There was even a road leading in, not the usual native footpath.

As we passed the outer huts natives popped out to look. They did not give us that scared, surprised stare most natives do when they see a car or white man come near their home. Here they were used to it. And the dozens of children didn't have drawn, underfed faces that plead with you; they were fat and healthy and happy. There was a definite atmosphere of native aristocracy, the well-built huts, the way they converged in concentric circles around the main hut, the many proud looking natives milling about. I became a little uneasy as I slowed the car to a stop some distance from Mtubatuba's hut. It wasn't the place itself — that I rather enjoyed — but the fact that I needed this chief's okay for any future plans made me a bit nervous. His nod might mean a whole new mission station reaping hundreds and thousands of Catholics in years to come. His no would mean we did nothing.

The Nduna in the back seat directed me to park the car about fifty yards from the chief's hut. It was easy to distinguish his hut from the many others by its size and fine decorative thatch. Again my man Thomas told me to stay in the car until called; he and Nduna would go in first. They got out and slowly walked to a spot halfway between the hut and the car. There visitors wait until summoned, and there they sat motionless and noiseless for one hour. I thought that's a long time for any native to keep a white man waiting — it's just not done in South Africa — but then this Mtubatuba isn't just any native. And I'd camp there for days if it would get us a site.

The time went fast for me in the car, the surroundings were so strange and interesting. In front of the chief's hut there was a striking native man prancing up and down enthusiastically, sputtering a continuous flow of Zulu with his deep, booming voice. He was the man whose job it is to stay near the chief at all times shouting his praises. He was tall, well built, good looking, and had a proud, graceful carriage. His clothing was warrior's garb, which is nothing but a piece of animal skin loincloth tied by a leather thong; a bikini is modest by comparison. He never stopped: "This is Chief Mtubatuba, son of chief so and so, who fought on the plains of ——, killed so many hundred of the —— tribe, whose cattle are numerous, whose words are fire, whose temper is fierce, whose wisdom . . ." and on and on. Often he would become worked up and shout: "Is this not the truth, men of Zulu?" "Yebo," everyone within hearing would automatically answer.

This bush-barker was a great distraction. But not any greater one than the many young, healthy, highly attractive, scantily clad native women and girls around the place. Remember, this is pagan country, and this old gay blade Mtubatuba sets the pace. These custom-built Salomes waltzed around by the dozens, munching on sticks of sugar cane, carrying water, popping in and out of huts; they kidded clumsily among themselves, bursting with loud guffaws, as they joked with the many eager men squatting around. These girls were living at the chief's kraal for one purpose, and obviously they knew it. They were bold, confident, but nonrepellent. Their every look and movement was a sexy one.

Finally, Thomas and the Nduna were summoned into Mtubatuba's hut, and ten minutes later they emerged to call me. I felt self-conscious getting out of the car and walking alone across the open space in front of the hut, every eye scrutinizing me as only native eyes can. I heard muffled giggles and whispers from the groups of girls, and was happy I couldn't catch their Zulu.

Leading to the hut was a narrow passage of bamboo poles about ten yards long. The entrance was extremely low cut, purposely, so that one entering would have to kneel first. I got down on my knees on the buckskin threshold and put my head inside. It was total darkness. My back blocked the only light. I paused there waiting for my eyes to adjust themselves. Not a sound was made while I peered into the blackness; I knew they were all looking at me and could see me well. I saw nothing for about a minute, just blinked and waited. Soon forms appeared along the circular walls, men, about twenty of them, sitting very still, legs crossed, heads bent forward watching me.

There were no women. The floor was covered with animal skins, some thick and furry. I looked along the line of men, trying to pick out the chief and the position I would take for our visit. He was not hard to distinguish. He sat apart from the rest of the men, away from the wall. His posture too was different: skinny bony knees pulled up in front of his sunken chest, he squatted on a skin of rich white fur. There was a chair on his left, the only one in the hut, obviously for me. As slowly and calmly as I could I went to it. Zulus seldom move quickly inside the hut; everything is done easily and effortlessly. I too tried to act nonchalant and respectful. Not a sound was made by anybody, nor did I say a word. The elders of the tribe were absorbed in this young, white, crew-cut Umfundisi.

Native protocol asks for a long pause and a long look at one another before greeting. When I got settled on the chair I slowly looked along the line of men, meeting each pair of eyes very gently. Then I looked at the chief. His head was about a yard away on my right, just waist high to me. He was an old man, perhaps ninety, with a long, thin, leathery face and extremely keen eyes. I waited for his greeting, since it was his place to speak first, but it never came. He caught my eye, looked at me appraisingly for a few seconds, waved his hand and turned away. Still not a sound. The silence was terribly uncomfortable for me.

Thomas spoke up to me in a whisper telling me to leave. I thought I misunderstood his Zulu, so he repeated, "Leave now, Father, there is no more for you here." He knows best about these things, so I got up and left. I came outside feeling like a beat dog, kicked to kennel for meddling. Chalk up another young priest's boner, I thought to myself, I still have a priority on them. The chief didn't even talk to me, didn't even greet me, how would he ever grant me land! Why he hardly looked at me. The whole visit took less than five minutes, five minutes I had evidently muffed somehow.

Back to the car I went, head down, without even looking at

the natives. It was a long, unpleasant wait for Thomas to come out and tell me of Mtubatuba's refusal. I sank into a philosophical mood looking out the window of our modern American car at all this primitive African paganism: These people are His, this country is His, I'm His — why must He let the advance of His Church hang on the whims of a moody native chief!

One look at Thomas' face said either he had taken plenty of native beer, or the chief said yes. He was beaming. Some of the other Ndunas came over to the car to say good-by. They were all smiling, but I have learned natives smile easily at white men. I shook hands with the men, gave a friendly wave to the fair sex, and drove off, anxious to get away and question Thomas.

Before I had asked, he came out with a Zulu word meaning we would probably get the site. He repeated it excitedly, and laughed at my dejection. "But the chief chased me!" I said. "He didn't chase you, Father, he just wanted to see you, and that's all he did. He always does that, looks at a person and passes on the request. He wants us to come back and he'll tell us for sure about the site. He was pleased with us, Father, don't worry!"

It would be nice to report that on the next visit the chief gave us the new site, that he asked for instruction and baptism, and told his tribe to do likewise. A St. Francis Xavier or our own Servite, St. Philip Benizi, would have scored like that, but not yours truly. (My shirts are nylon, not hair!) The chief did become my friend. In fact, I think he grew to like me on subsequent visits. He kidded me about my youth, and even mentioned what a crazy and impossible thing this celibacy business was. I told him what a good eye he obviously had for the more gentle sex, but I would bet he had his own troubles keeping peace among all of them. The old boy chuckled.

Our request for the site was granted as far as he was concerned, especially since the local Nduna pushed for it too. I thanked him sincerely, told him that now I would take it further — to the government authorities. And there is where it got bogged down, where it was smothered completely in heaps of red tape. Even now, years later, tons of technicalities still lie on it.

Once a month the natives around our Good Shepherd Mission in Hlabisa get treated to a laugh by the Umfundisi. It's a quiet sort of laugh they have on me, which takes place the day I pack our small panel van for a three-day stand at one of our oldest and most Catholic outstations. I say most Catholic because it has the greatest number of catechumens. To see me load up you would think I was on my way to the Kalahari Desert for life. The natives give me a willing hand with the luggage, but I know under their solemn faces there is a great pressure of laughter. They travel weeks with nothing but a stick and a loincloth, and I fill a one-ton truck with my stuff for three days out. I sometimes catch them smiling as they hand me things: stretcher bed, two-burner stove, lamp, folding chair, bundles of blankets, and a huge case of food. This, and the ever-present Mass kit.

The first time I visited this outstation the natives thought me quite normal, because I took two blankets, sandwiches, and some water. Since then I have discovered I'm no Daniel Boone (except that I always need a haircut), and I don't mind the parishioners laughing at me. I try to bring as much comfort as I can to this desolate place. And I never did go in for boyscouting.

The name of the outstation is Matchamhlope, Zulu for "white rocks." Years ago some priest approached the chief about it, got his okay; went through government red tape, got theirs, and then started to work. It's about thirty miles from home, up a winding, treacherous mountain road. Our tough vehicles take a beating making it. Before you arrive at the top, which is a huge rock towering over the surrounding hills, you reach our small church, about the size of a two-car garage. It's the oldest mission station in the area, and that you never doubt. In the early 1920's German Benedictines built it out of mud, rocks, and anything else they could find. It's falling apart now because the government has forbidden repairs to it. The four windows are out, the walls are cracking, the cow-dung floor is sinking, and the roof is a sieve.

On the first day of an outstation visit, the idea is to make as much noise as possible to let the people know you're there. Coming up I wave, toot the horn, and stop all I see to tell them Mass will be there tomorrow and the next day. I send word to the local catechist to come right away, and continue on up to the church. There I unload the gear into the church, all except the stretcher bed. That's set up in the van. One night I slept in the church, but the mice and bats and lizards convinced me I had not chosen the better part.

On one of my early visits to the Matchamhlope outstation a fierce rain started beating down when I arrived. Tropical rains are relentless. There was not a chance to walk around and visit the natives, yet I could not go back to the Mission; the road had been washed out in two places. So I sat in the panel van, a chilly but dry home, hunched over the steering wheel, scribbling.

One morning I overslept. Padres land into some real fixes by oversleeping, but few get what I did. Mass was scheduled for about seven. The rattling rain on the steel roof of the small van did not wake me until eight. Through the dripping windshield I could see no one around, and expected to say Mass alone. I ran through the rain into the church, burst in upon fifteen people sitting on the floor waiting for me. They were drenched and smiling, I was sleepy-eyed and embarrassed in my undershirt. I tried to be at ease and make a Zulu joke about them waking up their Umfundisi, but like most of my jokes, it just lay there.

There are no pews in the church, and the one table in front is used for Mass, for cooking, and for washing. I used it in my morning toilet: I went about washing, shaving, cleaning my teeth while they looked on, fascinated. A little girl giggled when I cut myself shaving: in my crankiness I felt like asking her to do better with cold water and no mirror. The toothbrush and my funny faces while using it enthralled them.

The older missionaries who did the spade work here would be pleased to see that small, soaking congregation — fruit of their labor. It's a rinky-dink church on a windswept mountain, but let any priest stop here for Mass, and he is sure to gather handfuls of fervent, religion-starved Catholics. Before Mass there are confessions. Usually all the people wait outside and come in one by one; this morning, because of the rain, I went out in the van and heard there so they could remain in the church. When Mass begins they sing their beautiful, rhythmic, melancholy Zulu hymns. The dilapidated structure becomes a sanctuary. But I had little opportunity for pious contrasts, the rain dripped on the altar forcing me to move it.

When the weather is nice, and it usually is, the catechist and I leave after Mass to visit the huts. This visiting, dull and trying as it often is, is the very heart of our job. This is how you learn the local gossip, break into the serenely simple lives of these natives, listen to endless complaints about the rain, the sun, the crops. Natives are born moaners, but happy ones. On these visits too, in hushed tones, the people tell the priest about the wives who ran off, the husbands who got drunk, and the teen-agers who got caught. In and out of those dark, low entrances you go, seeing Catholics, Protestants, pagans; trying not to slight anyone, because natives are highly sensitive and a priest's visit is not taken lightly.

As the sun goes down and my legs follow suit I send the catechist home and continue on to my hermitage church for supper. This is a trying time for me, mainly because I'm no cook, and I'm tired and hungry. When I began cooking for myself I had ideas of doing things properly, soup, vegetables, meat, and the rest, all done on time, nicely. I was a total failure, and an angry man. No two things would be warm at the right time, though I had two good burners. The soup was cold when the meat was hot. Cool the potatoes and the coffee would boil

over. Everything going on at once made me nervous. I'd burn
a finger, spill something, then loose my temper and my appetite.
Now things are different. I open one can, heat it and eat it.
Cut the bread, butter it, and eat it. Make coffee, drink it. . . .
Talk about Solomon!

While stationed at Good Shepherd Mission I struck upon
another way of reaching distant areas, by means of a sort of a
portable outstation. Tent-Service would be a name for it. Out-
wardly it's not much different from the camp meetings and
religious revivals of the olden Middle West. There is the tent,
the preacher, the open field, the heterogeneous crowd. But block
the comparison quickly. We have the Mass, Truth, a genuine
priest, and very little unbalanced emotion.

In much of our territory, as I have indicated, there is not a
chance to get a site for a school. Yet the area is filled with
children, children who could board at the mission and become
educated Catholics. You can't just go around picking up boarding children for the asking. Native parents in these outlying
districts are suspicious of reading and writing; they never had
it, and neither will their children. Still, if they are approached
properly and told clearly about school, many parents will agree
to having their children stay at the mission.

For this approaching and explanation you need time with
them. And that's how the tent idea was born. With it the
priest can go into any area he pleases, stay for a few days visiting parents, recruiting kids, having daily Mass, and even setting
up catechism classes. Two or three days a month in some area
over a period of a year can acquaint a lot of people with the
Catholic Church, and acquaint them effectively, so that they
want to study the catechism and want to be baptized, and want
to worship God in the proper way.

This camping out doesn't come easy to a city kid from
Chicago's west side; I've got bruises to show. The very first
night I ever spent in a tent was the worst. After the catechist and

I had got it set up, and he had gone off to sleep in a nearby native kraal, the inevitable rain came. I suddenly found myself trying to do ten things at once. The kerosene stove blew out with the first gust of wind. I ran to tie the flaps down and got soaked to the skin in seconds. I kicked my shins painfully on a tent stake as I scrambled in. The stretcher bed and blankets were high and dry but my two loaves of bread were sopping in inches of water. The flashlight stopped working when I used it to pound a stake. I dug a hand into the Mass kit for a candle and knocked the vestments into the dirty water on the floor. . . . My mutterings weren't aspirations!

I ate cold beans and watery bread in the cramped, dark space beneath the sagging canvas. The dishwashing problem that night was nil — I left the empty tin cans floating on the floor. Wind threatened the tent but never quite won. Out in this bush at night, alone in a tent, you would think a newcomer such as I was would be more afraid of snakes than anything else. But I wasn't afraid of snakes that night. I felt that they would drown themselves getting to me.

Now that I've been making these monthly camping trips to different areas for some time, I have an efficient routine, which eliminates a lot of wasted effort and a lot of unnecessary discomfort. In fact, these trips can be pleasant, especially in the late afternoon about an hour before dark. I put my camp chair in front of the tent, slump in it completely relaxed after the busy day, light up a cigar, cross my legs, and puff pensively. And I have learned the few simple precautions to take against getting wet by rain. If only some of the guys back home could see me! If only I could tell them how it feels deep inside to come up to this lonely loft of a mountain for a few days and celebrate Mass for these simple, raw, likable pagans. If only I could slice off a half hour, and pass it on to them so they could experience this other world the African natives live in!

Kids only are around me now, as I sit here; and the thick, fragrant cigar smoke curls lazily overhead into the shady

branches of a low-hanging thorn tree. They are happy puffs
without a breeze to scatter them. From the kids you grasp
that other-world contrast. They're always at my tent, from the
time they hear the jeep laboring over the last hill until they
see my pockets emptied of candy. At first they were shy and
reticent, wouldn't come near the white man who "carries his
home with him." But now they are used to me. Many of their
playmates have already been boarding with us at the mission.

It's a treat to sit here and catch the conversation around me.
It seldom stops. They never saw a cigar before. One pipes up
to his tiny friend, "Look at that big tobacco stick — it fills his
whole mouth!" They giggle and watch me. I go along with
their joke (they're happy to see a white man laugh with them
and not at them) and ask how their daddy takes his tobacco.
One game lad pulls out his lower lip, inserts a dirty paw
deeply in front of his lower teeth, and says: "This is the place
for daddy's tobacco, and mommy's too."

At arms' reach from me two more little guys are sitting at
the door of the tent, afraid to step in but stretching their necks
to look. "No, he doesn't sleep down here, he sleeps on those
sticks," pointing to the stretcher bed. "And you don't know, but
I know what that is for," turning a pudgy finger to the kerosene
burner. "He cooks with the little fire inside. No, you silly, he
doesn't gather wood, it just burns. I saw it work last moon when
he was here."

Ten yards in front of me the jeep is parked under a tree.
On the tailgate is a basin of water, dirty now with the dust of
my face and hands. Kids are climbing over the jeep in ecstasies
of excitement, jumping on the seats, drumming on the hood,
staring into the rear-view mirror. No danger of them harming
anything, our jeep is rugged with no delicate accessories. Those
on the hood get their drumming into a rhythm as only natives
can. Two little girls about seven and eight years old pick up
the beat and go into a shuffling dance. Not soft-shoe, but its
ancestor. The steady beating brings the other kids into a circle

of clapping hands around the two girls. I call for them to move aside so I too can watch, give a few out-of-time claps myself and tell them to carry on. That's all they wanted, ecclesiastical approval.

With large grins and lively kicks the two hoofers react spontaneously to the audience. The rags they're wearing encumber free movement so they tear them off and leave only a string of beads around their waists. The clapping tempo increases and their movement with it, effortlessly. Their small, lithe bodies sway loose and easy with the claps. Dancing is in native blood. I puff on calmly with a benign smile. The kids are happy, I'm contented. Not half bad, this missionary life.

Suddenly I'm jolted out of these soothing reveries. I sit up unbelievingly, blink my eyes. Gulp in heavy smoke and almost swallow the cigar! Right in front of me, nonchalantly as you please, the two little sirens swing their tiny hips into the unmistakable movements of bumps and grinds! A couple of Minsky's maidens! Nervously I champ at the cigar. They know nothing about nothing, these kids, just copying what they saw, I know, but copying with perfection. I can't give anything away by looking strange. I don't want any rock around my neck for scandalizing His precious little ones. And I dare not stop them; they'll get suspicious. Children are quick about those things. So I make an herculean effort to look natural, puff more rapidly, whistle, yawn, and squirm. The brash little tykes — that stuff is dynamite!

The weather and kid's caprices change quickly. The sun dips under the mountain and a damp chill moves in. One of the children suggest a fire, I agree, and in a few minutes it's blazing in front of the tent. Natives are experts with fire. They huddle around it, and I pull my chair up too.

Often when I have the kids hanging around like this I teach them phrases of the Hail Mary or Our Father. They like it for a few minutes. But today it would be poor timing. They are in no Hail Mary mood. There's a little nine-year-old wise guy holding forth about how much cattle he would never give to marry the local debs. Wives are bought with cattle among the natives. This dowry, or exchange of cattle for a girl, is called a *Lobola*. The nine-year-old just told the haughty little miss across the fire from him that he would not even consider chancing two goats on her; she made a face and didn't like the way we all laughed at her. I went to pat her tufty head, and she tossed it up femininely and moved away.

Since prayers are out today, I try a plug for school, telling them the glories of three meals a day, kicking a football, writing down marks that speak. Some of them are horrified at the suggestion of school, and you can hardly blame them. They have an easy, carefree time here and all they hear about school are horror stories, whacks from the teacher, being boxed up in a room all day, no hunting animals of either category. Of course, that ride in Father's jeep at the beginning and end of the school year would be nice, but all considered, this school business is a risk.

Our two dancing girls are interested in school because once upon a time they saw the colorful dresses worn by school girls. But they tell me they haven't a chance — their father won't agree. "But if you ask him nicely, with tears?" and here I gesture two rivers of tears from my eyes — a bit of ham that always gets a laugh. "We do, but he socks us," they reply.

My cigar is out. Without a word one of the girls quietly reaches to the fire, takes out an ember, blows on it, and presents it to me with two hands and a little curtsy. They may be coarse, but don't tell me primitive people have no natural and charming politeness about them. Our Zulus are full of it. I thank her, she bows gracefully with the sleeping baby strapped on her back, and I light up. (Ah, you must wonder where bush missionaries in dark Africa get cigars! Just remember that American, Chicago Catholics are the most thoughtful and generous in the world, and well-packed cigars travel oceans and equators intact.)

The potatoes I had put on the little burner are now done, I can hear the muffled boiling inside the tent. The kids are quiet. The fire is low. It's getting dark. There is just enough candy in my pocket to go around. Such accuracy comes with practice. They perk up as my hand digs in; nothing like a native kid's face when candy is coming. A final warning for them to be around for Mass and catechism in the morning. I get each one to promise individually, then I send them all home by pretending to reach for a switch.

"Stay well, Umfundisi," they call back to me. "Go well, children." I pitch the cigar butt into the ashes and hustle in to those spuds.

4. Natives at Play

MY EYES were getting used to the dark. Pupils had dilated and were adjusting themselves to see more of this hidden, shadowy, wonder world of the African native. The language barrier was receding, and I began to realize how blinded a new missionary is until he gets over that first hurdle of Zulu speech. Conversation, even with the older people whose speech is fast and careless, was becoming effortless. And here at Good Shepherd Mission in the heart of Zululand only the purest Zulu is spoken.

Each day brought a deeper insight into the lives of these people. Not so much when they came to me at the mission, but when I went to their homes. At the mission they were out of their element; they were on white-man's property, even though that of a friendly missionary. They knocked on the door, spoke their piece, made their request, said good-by. They were reserved. In their own surroundings, at their individual kraals, they were different entirely. At home, around their fires, they were relaxed, themselves; they had no care for white-man protocol. This was especially true when they let their hair down to have fun. And, believe me, these Zulus know how to have fun. They seem to be the happiest people in the world.

One day the catechist and I had been out in a five-mile perimeter combing the bush for new catechumens, new school children. We had to walk because the jeep was too large for these narrow paths. We were tired as we trudged along in the late afternoon. Our gait was steady but slow, my companion in front carrying the empty lunch bag and I behind with my walking stick. Neither of us spoke. We had been out all day and our wells of chatter were dry. The bush was silent and breathless. The soft sand swooshed under our feet; the loose top on the thermos bottle clacked out a montonous rhythm as it bounced against the catechist. What he was thinking about, God only knows. He created the inscrutable native. My thoughts were on cold American beer, one inch of foam on it and in a tall frosted glass.

From the distance there came a faint and regular thumping. As we walked on, coming closer to its origin, the sound seemed to fill the countryside. This sound of drums is not an unfamiliar one in the bush, day or night, but the great volume of sound that we now heard was rare. We rounded a hill and a large kraal crowded with colorfully dressed natives came into view. My first thought was that this was a prayer meeting of some native Protestant sect. The catechist quickly sized it up as a wedding. The large number of people is what attracted my interest. All day I had met perhaps fifty people, now here were five or six hundred waiting to be smitten by the sight of a Roman collar.

The drums stopped and a sudden silence came over them as they spotted me and whispered, "There's a white man." It was easy to smile calmly at the galleries of startled black faces. From experience I knew that the genuine smile of a white man has disarming power with them. But it must be genuine — their eyes are keen at spotting falsity. The headman came up and greeted me ceremoniously. He was an elderly man with an agreeable face, a gracious manner — and a terrific odor. He held well all the native beer he had drunk. I explained who I was and asked to rest a while and watch the wedding dances of his people. He was thrilled with the request, said I was the first white man ever to enter his yard. A woman was ordered to bring me a homemade chair, rickety but comfortable after our walking. He set it under a shady tree at one end of the yard then sat down on the ground next to me. We had a perfect view of everything.

I had seen many native dances before, but almost always at some kind of a show, a school affair, government display, craftwork exhibition, etc. There the natives dressed for the occasion, danced their dance, and it was over. The thing had a false, play-acting ring to it. This was nothing of the kind. Here was a real pagan wedding in one of the most primitive areas of South Africa. These natives were not showing off for appreciative Europeans, they were performing ancient tribal ceremonies. These were ritual wedding dances done in dead seriousness.

The headman gave the signal to resume. Drums took up the beat at one corner of the yard on our left; there were about ten women pounding them with their bare hands. It was a lively rhythm, not unlike our boogie beats. The deep guttural voices of the men rolled in heavily with their mumbo-jumbo chant. They dragged out vowels in a hollow wail, then suddenly clipped them short with a hiss. Women wove in their high falsettos. Children clapped their hands with subdued reverence. Everyone meshed with the contagious rhythm. In ten minutes the huge yard was resounding with other-world noises.

The men's group called and chanted back and forth to one another in powerful bass voices. Women shrieked high prolonged, controlled screams. The five or six hundred people jived and shrugged in effortless unison. Suddenly all vocal sounds stopped and you could hear only the hushed drums and a thousand bare feet shuffling softly together, patting the dust lightly. As they beat out the muffled rhythm without a word, the unity was unbelievable. Then the crescendo increased, the steps became stamps, the dust rose to their knees, their heels became hammers pounding the earth. Emotion swelled through the crowd as it worked itself into a frenzy of measured motion. I could feel the violent thumping through the legs of my chair. A strange feeling came over me in the rhythmic din. It is at such rare and fleeting moments that the missionary gets a jolting realization of the immensity of his work. He watches almost fearfully the stark paganism before him, the gaping ignorance, the appalling primitiveness of these simple people. They are centuries behind. They haven't a clue to the outside, Christian, cultured world. And he, little he, is their only contact with the greater realities. Where does he begin?

The young men now formed a large moving circle in the yard. They were dressed in fancy loincloths which showed off their muscular thighs, smooth and oiled. They carried spears, sticks, and shields. Each one would jump into the center and narrate some little ditty to the others. As he did this with shouts and grotesque leaps into the air, he would gnash his teeth, roll his eyes, thrust violently with the spear. The chorus, meanwhile, in sonorous harmony urged him on in the tale. When he finished another would jump in and tell his story. I could not catch all the Zulu words, but I can assure you they weren't dealing with the lives of the saints.

Next to the men was a larger and more interesting circle of women. Though not as boisterous as the men, the women were more in the mood. A few wore European dresses, but the majority had nothing but a half-tied skirt and scanty blouse if any at all. They were perfectly preened, native style: shiny black skin, bright beads and earrings, gaudy handkerchiefs around their heads. Their dancing was slower, more graceful, its cadence charged with sinuous explosiveness. Two or three attractive ones entered the large center and led the others. They would decide when to change steps, and all would follow. Each different step meant something because at each change the onlooking men would howl like wolves, and the women would answer with a knowing grin. The only ones in the yard who did not catch the innuendo of the ritual wedding dances were the children under ten.

Except for an occasional word to my catechist I sat there in absorbed silence. So would you or any other white man, it was so strange. I wasn't dreaming, wasn't reading a tall tale of Dr. Livingston; I was not sitting in the Chicago Theatre watching "African Drums" or some other hair-raiser. This was real, and I was here. Me, the same west side Chicago kid who had shined shoes in Madison Street taverns for a nickel a shine. And now here I was in Africa with a new job: these jumping, jiving, dirty, noisy, crazy-eyed black people were it!

An hour went by before I realized how late it was. I must figure some graceful way to leave: a short speech to the crowd, a few kind words to the headman, a public prayer for the newly-weds, any of these would do, as I had proved before.

Here I decided to try something different, hoping thereby to ingratiate myself and Company with the whole tribe. If it worked, my words might have more weight later, when I asked about church. A one-pound note is a lot of money to a native, sometimes a month's salary — about three American dollars. I told the catechist to present a pound note to each of the newly-weds as a gift from the priest of the Roman Church in their area. He was not to make his usual sales talk for worshiping God; just present the gift and briefly tell its source. Then we would leave.

The catechist approached the headman, who stopped the dancing and got everyone's attention. Ceremoniously the cate-chist placed the crisp notes in the hands of the husband and wife. They looked like teen-agers. While all listened in stunned silence he used about three simple sentences to tell them the why and wherefore of the gift. All eyes turned on me, open consterna-tion on their faces — such a gift from an unknown white man! Oh's and ah's came from every side.

They interpreted the gift to the couple as a gift to themselves, and were thrilled. If they only knew what greater things I could channel to them! Maybe someday they would. The headman told them with a loud voice that they should all thank me together. There was a pause. Then five hundred mellow voices, pitched with sincerity, together, and with the simplicity that is a delight to the missionary, said the soft Zulu words, "Siyabonga, Umfundisi."

All native weddings, all pagan play, is not as pleasant as that episode. Often and easily the vicious, animal side of the native bursts out at their gatherings. One Saturday afternoon as I was sitting alone at the Good Shepherd Mission enjoying the quiet of the empty school and wishing for the Notre Dame game on the radio, the native cook boy bounded in sweating and breathless. "Oh, Father, these natives!" He could hardly speak from excitement. His eyes popped and he shook all over while I got the story out of him.

He had been to a relative's wedding that morning. I knew the place, about two miles into the reserve, on top of a hill. It was a pagan kraal, rawest of the raw. All morning I had seen little groups of people passing in that direction. The Christians were dressed in their best church clothes, while the pagans sported scanty brightly colored animal skins, their bare black bodies glistening with grease. The young men carried choice knobkerries — long, well-carved sticks with a heavy knob of hard wood at one end, which they use in a fight instead of fists. The idea is to hit the other's head with the knob end. They dance and shout and edge for position, then swing. One blow can be fatal.

The wedding had got off to a roaring start the night before. All night long we could hear them from the mission — distant drums and the rhythmic rumble of their tireless singing. With the morning came the ceremony of exchanging the cattle for the girl. There was plenty of food and native beer. About noon the young warriors began to feel their oats. The beer, the heat, the sensual dances and songs, the admiring women, all combined to urge them on. One began to show his prowess with a knobkerrie. Another buck stepped in. Factions formed, and soon the kraal yard was a seething mass of blood-crazy natives. The women rushed for cover, the men swung with reckless abandon. Our cook boy made a hurried exit. Before he left, two men were lying dead with crushed skulls.

I had no intention of going over — I value my head — but

I did climb to a nearby hill and look across. From my perch I could not see much, just a milling mob of excited natives. Some were coming away from the center of the fighting circle. Many ran to the outer edge, then turned and went back at it. The one white policeman in the area would not approach the hill. In fact, he was doing the same thing I was, looking on from a safe distance. He had already sent for reinforcements. A half dozen police could handle it, but it would be foolish for one to try. Natives have a healthy respect for white skin, especially the white skin of a policeman. But a drinking native is unpredictable, and prudent whites keep that fact very much in mind.

Later in the afternoon a local chief came to me for a favor. He was the picture of sorrow, as were the aids around him. They had not been in the fight, but had heard about it. Now they were summoned by the police to clean up. There were five men dead, many hurt, would I please haul two of the bodies to the chief's home for burial. They were two of his best men. I knew it would be a nasty job, and this chief was strictly a phony who deserved no favors, but I agreed. Odd jobs like this sometimes pay off big dividends — sometimes.

The five bodies had been brought to the small police station for a cursory examination as to the cause of death. It wasn't hard to figure out. As I looked down at them I thought of the gory Indian stories I read as a kid. Huge, fine, muscular black bodies, decorated with colorful beads and bright furry loincloths, lying in pools of their own odorous blood, their skulls crushed beyond recognition. One crashing blow of a knobkerrie and it's all over. They had received that blow plus. These skulls and faces could not have been so completely pulverized while the man was on his feet. After he went down, hot, beastly ferocity spent itself in an orgasm of savagery. What a dreadful sound those final blows must have made as they thudded home!

Native constables and I respectfully wrapped the two bodies in blankets and loaded them into our panel van. The chief got in along with a few semihysterical women. The stench from the mangled bodies was fierce. I opened all windows but it didn't help. Fifteen minutes of driving and I felt faint; one of the women had already passed out. We had an hour's drive ahead; the bumpy road jostled the limp bodies. For my sake the chief kept the mourning women down to a low moan. Occasionally there was a screechy wail, but not often; the chief carried a stick and would not hesitate to use it on a crying woman. On the way we saw a rhino, which is a rare sight. I mentioned it, but not a head turned. The awful odor and catastrophe of violent death dominated everything.

Arrived at the kraal, the chief got out and solemnly walked ahead of our hearse. Handfuls of people came from different directions, and stood around staring wide-eyed at the priest and van. They all knew what had happened; news travels fast in the bush. Some began mourning out loud, but a sharp look from the chief and they stopped. He perhaps thought I was opposed to open mourning and for that reason would have none of it. He even reprimanded a cute little girl who came up and grinned at me. I took her hand and told him it was all right for her to smile, she didn't understand what had happened.

We unloaded the bodies into the nicest hut and carefully laid them in the center. My hands were moist and reddish from handling the blankets. The people entered the hut after us and gathered around waiting for me to make the next move. I wanted to pray for them but I had to come out for air first. Back in again I went for a few quick Hail Mary's in Zulu. The people were quiet and respectful, but I had to answer the prayers myself, none of them had ever heard such jibberish before. I shook hands all around and was overwhelmed with their thanks. The chief too expressed gratitude, but his was false. False, because the next time I visited him, he would not even see me.

What is the outcome of such an affair? (And they are not infrequent.) The natives talk about it for a while and it's soon forgotten. On the police blotter it's simply a "Faction Fight," one minor family against another. But they don't pass over it lightly; they can't afford to. The police try to round up all who took part in it. Native constables get the names from informers. For this one, they had a list of over a hundred and twenty men. When sixty were gathered, trial was held. Various sentences were given, ranging from two months, to three years, hard labor. All sixty got something.

Effects of it kicked back on our own moderate building program. Brother John Bardini, the lay brother from Italy, was building an additional classroom onto the school. He had about ten native laborers. The Monday after the fight not one of his men showed up for work — they were all in jail. John lost a week getting a new crew.

Christmas is another great playtime period for the natives. "Kiss-ee-moo-zi" is the Zulu for it. No matter how deep you penetrate into the bush, mention Kiss-ee-moo-zi and faces light up. Old pagans, wearing strings of broken teeth around their necks, reeking with superstitions — and just plain reeking — want to know when Christmas is this year. Only a few churchgoers know its true meaning. Every other native knows it as a time when white people trade gifts and a time when missionaries throw a feast for their parishioners.

Only in its essence is Christmas in Africa like ours at home. It's the hottest part of the year, midsummer. All vegetation has a deep, lush, sensuous green; foliage is at its thickest. The sun is bright and close and killing. The air is still and heavy. You are always changing clothes.

At the growing Good Shepherd Mission we decided to have an all-out Christmas for two reasons: Celebration of Christ's Birthday itself and publicity for our school. We figured now was the time to make a big splash in order to get children for the new school year beginning in February. The splash was to be in the form of food. Slaughter a cow, cook up pots of meat and porridge, and invite the whole area, giving Catholics preference. Let them all fill their stomachs and then plug for the school.

The slaughtering of a cow is an important event with the Zulus. Any feast is a flop if there is not plenty of meat to go around. Meat is not in their regular diet, so they look on it as a great treat. It's the man's task to kill the cow with his spear, cut it properly into cookable chunks, and set them aside. Every native man knows the job well and revels in it. Then the women put the meat into large three legged black iron pots, add water and native seasoning (indigenous hot peppery berries, herbs, peppers), and kindle a steady fire under the pot.

I bought a cow from a local native, for about thirty-five dollars in American money, and the day before Christmas I decided to shoot her myself instead of letting the men kill her with spears. Natives are eager for a laugh on their priest, and when I take a gun into my hands, they get it. One shot should have finished this tired old beast, chewing her cud in the hot sun — one shot especially at five yards. I emptied the .38 revolver before the cow even took her big, sad, googly eyes off me. When she finally went down, the three or four men I had selected for the cutting job went at it with a will.

There are no deep freezers down here, and the cut-up meat will only last one day in this tropical climate. Early the following morning, Christmas, some of our chosen women parisioners were on hand to do the cooking. There was actually no work for me to do personally except to pull the trigger (six times, however!) and organize the men and women to help.

My schedule for Christmas might have been called "Operation Spread Out": Midnight Mass at one small outstation, seven in the morning at another, then the main Mass at home at about eleven. Both the outstation Masses were like Masses at outstations usually are: disappointing attendance and tiresome traveling. An outstation never satisfies a missionary until it graduates and receives its "diploma" — a resident priest.

The Christmas Mass and feast at home were deeply gratifying.

When I drove in at about ten in the morning our yard was crowded. Now, I thought, this is more like Christmas. It was even a holiday-looking crowd, African style. All were dressed in their best. Boys with clean shirts and tidy short pants. Old women with well-ironed dresses unencumbered with the usual odd pockets and straps and dirty snuff bottles hanging on. For the girls and young women Christmas is like our Easter Parade; they dress to kill. And after you have been here a while you think they don't do so badly either. Garish combinations galore, clashing colors shouting at one another, but clean and odorless. They wear bright, flowery house dresses and fill them very well indeed.

The bush seemed to have emptied itself of Catholics. I had a long line of confessions, and wouldn't want a better way to foul up the schedule. The schoolroom church looked like a cartoon drawing. It was jammed. Kids had their heads out the windows, crying and gasping for air. Women pushed and puffed and squatted. Our busy-boy ushers were in their glory, and quite useless. The head usher, who had just been appointed by me to that honor the day before and was thrilled with it, was a little old guy with one eye and a lot of courage; he kept getting his blind side bludgeoned with elbows. He would turn furiously and the offending elbow would be gone. Brother John had been busy all morning directing the women in the kitchen. They are good, they know their job, but they need constant surveillance, and John is a master at it. If it were not for his steady help, along with that of the experienced catechist, I never could have managed a "Kiss-ee-moo-si" feast for so many. The veranda was crowded too. Here sat the merely curious and those who came for food only. They did not know or care about church, and they already had plenty of native beer in them. They were raw pagans scantily dressed in animal skins, whom I was glad to have there; but I did wish God would send an occasional breeze across that veranda.

Elbowing my way up to the altar at Mass time I chucked

baby chins, patted kids' heads, gently toed bulky, well-planted women out of the way. Arrived at the front table, I found all the essentials there, liturgical enough, but I would have to remove that cute baby from the missal stand before beginning; her dangling feet were dirtying the altar cloth. She protested loudly, but I squared things by letting her play with the tassels of my cincture while I vested. Wapelhorst writhed.

The packed room was intolerably hot. Even the natives were suffering. Babies gave forth that intense, violent, angry yowling that must have relief. Mothers could not take them out because they couldn't get out. They stuffed a variety of things into their babies' mouths and blew on their faces. Men wilted in their unfamiliar clothes. Fat women were pitiful. Everyone shifted uncomfortably. And to this hushed pandemonium I turned around, dripping with sweat from the heavy vestments, little Zulu Gospel book in hand, little voice in my parched throat, and tried to read the story of Christmas as St. John recorded it. No room in the inn!

My prepared sermon with introduction, meat, and close was out of the question. I began at the top of my voice and shouted my lungs out, mustering all the Zulu I knew to get over the essential elements of Bethlehem. But the faces, far from showing interest, pleaded with me to finish and get on with the Mass. I tried one "But let me put it another way," watched it belly-flop, then continued the Mass. Those curious pagans on the veranda got a good idea of "Kiss-ee-moo-zi" all right — something about Father Thomas delivering a baby in a stable somewhere on a very cold night.

When I bent over for the Consecration the wet vestments fell away from my chest and a hot blast of air hit me in the face. After this I heard my first Christmas carol of the year. And what an impression it made in that unique setting! The two hundred or more people behind me slowly wound up and confidently bellowed out the familiar "Silent Night." The tune was the same as ours, the words were Zulu. You can't match the natives for singing, and this hymn they know and love. Their controlled voices undulated easily over the simple melody. They dropped to silence, then swelled powerfully until the room vibrated with sound. I began the Pater Noster and got all mixed up: I was saying Latin, listening to Zulu, and thinking in English. Thinking about home and Christmas.

Because of the heat I thought of skipping Benediction. But the incense and profound bows might make a great impression on the pagans, in addition to the power of the blessing itself. One never knows how these things work. So we sweated through it. And after it the catechist wanted to harangue them, but I cut him short and announced dinner in the outer lobby. While they shuffled out in confusion and misery the mother of that cute baby placed the sleeping bundle back on the missal stand. I gave her a nod that it was okay, conditionally. She knew the condition.

Feasting the natives is one of the most enjoyable parts of Christmas for me. They were deliriously happy to be finished with that hot schoolroom church, and they knew those four huge smoking pots held plenty. Lines were quickly formed leading to the kitchen, where Brother John reigned. He's an old hand at this and knows how to control the natives nicely. A few looks and words, not necessarily sharp, and they're in the palm of his hand. I attempted to put order into the lines, but not much. This was no time for discipline. Instead, I merely floated around razzing the fat ones about their large tummies, urging the skinny ones to eat up (native humor must be obvious and horsy), and slipping pieces of candy to the kids. Each person got a chunk of meat, a dish of porridge, and a lot of soupish gravy over everything. The cow did not last long.

It was amusing to catch them sneaking in for seconds before they were through with their firsts. Old, broken-down, harmless-looking grandmothers would stick an unchewed bone into their wraps and limp into line for another. I'd reach to grab the hidden bone and they'd wrinkle their faces into a toothless grin and hobble off. The kids would hide their food in the bushes, then would come around for seconds. A look from John would send them scurrying.

By four in the afternoon all were fed and full. Every shady spot in the yard was taken up with sprawling, happy natives. "Kiss-ee-moo-zi" was over.

5. Black Helpers

IT TAKES a while for natives to get used to their missionary priest. They have to study him slowly, ever so slowly. Natives are never in a hurry. Circumstances on the mission lend themselves to this close scrutiny of the priest. The natives see him in the morning before Mass and coffee. They know his moods, watch his walk, clean his house, do his cooking, know what he's doing every hour of the day. There is a close, large-family spirit on the mission. And the priest in charge is the patriarch of all. He's respected, obeyed, and usually deeply loved.

This last is what makes changes difficult. Some of their simple, genuine affection is bound to rub off on the priest. And to be transferred from a mission after you have dug yourself in does not come easily. At Good Shepherd Mission in Hlabisa it was like that for me. I had been there a year, had become well acquainted with the people, knew their children, their fields, their cattle, their lives. And I had grown to love them and my work among them. The word from the Bishop for me to change came as a mild blow.

The Bishop's word was that I was to transfer back to our main house in Ingwavuma and take charge of that fast-growing mission, where I had first studied Zulu. It's a beautiful mission, Our Lady of Ingwavuma. The priest house is large, about fifteen rooms, and well built out of cement blocks. There is a native sisters' convent occupied by four Servite African sisters, a small school, boarding quarters, and a richly decorated chapel. This is the house where the new missionaries come to study Zulu for from six months to a year. That means there are always about six or seven men living there — plenty of company for a pinochle game in the dull quiet evenings.

It was here where I began to appreciate the wisdom of the words of Pope Pius XI in his encyclical on the missions, *Rerum Ecclesiae*. He is speaking of the need of a native clergy: "If you do not work with all your might to accomplish this [the establishment of a native clergy], We maintain that your apostolate will be not only crippled, but it will prove to be an obstacle and an impediment for the establishment and organization of the Church in those countries. . . . In order that you may be able to make more progress in winning over to Christ new converts from heathenism, shall it not help you greatly to be able to leave to the native clergy the parts already converted for them to guard and cultivate? Nay, even the native clergy will prove to be most useful, more useful in fact than it was ever imagined in extending more widely the Kingdom of Christ, 'for since the native priest' — to use the words of Our Predecessor — 'by birth and temper, by sentiment and by interests is in touch with his own people, it is marvelous how valuable he can be in instilling the Faith into the minds of his people.' He knows, in fact, better than anyone else, the best methods to follow; and so it frequently happens that he will often gain access where a foreign priest could never gain entrance. Moreover, foreign missionaries on account of their imperfect knowledge of the language are frequently prevented from expressing themselves. As a result the force and efficacy of their preaching are greatly weakened" (Para. 23).

South Africa is a black country. We white missionaries have been sent here not to run the Church, but to plant it. To bridge the gap between white and black is far harder for the missionary than for others here. Mining people, for instance, have native mine boss boys who carry instructions from the white front office to the black laborers in the hole, and the gold comes up efficiently. White farmers, with a little Zulu, can successfully farm thousands of acres and never lift a hay fork. Store people, garage mechanics, police, can all carry on their work with the help of natives and not bother much about bridging that white-black gap. And, indeed, why should they worry? Mining companies don't intend to turn their mines over to the natives eventually; farmers and storekeepers are not going to pass their lands or their businesses to anyone but their own heirs.

For us missionaries, however, it's essential that we cross this seeming abyss between white and black. Ours is not a white man's religion to be used by the blacks. What we want down here is literally Black Catholicism. Anything short of that is failure.

We deal in things of the mind and heart and will, not shovels and picks and forks. We have to get under the crust of the native with our wares; we must burrow deeply into their lives, touch the very core of their being, blast out paganism and lay in the Truth. That is why native helpers are so important to us. That is why we need good native bishops, priests, sisters, brothers, catechists, and teachers.

Here in the little world of the Ingwavuma Mission we are fortunate enough to have native sisters. They are from a native branch of the Servite Mantellate Sisters working in Swaziland and Zululand. And they are worth their weight in gold, these funny-looking, robed women with the black bare feet sticking out. One of these sisters here is an old warrior who has pulled me out of not a few awkward situations, one of which I remember particularly well.

A young man came asking for a boarding girl we have, saying her father needed the girl at home because he was sick. She was supposed to go back with him immediately. It would be a full day's walk to her home, and they would not reach there before dark. I was about to send the girl when this wise old sister hesitatingly came up and suggested that perhaps the girl was too tired to walk that far. I bluntly ruled that helping her sick father was more important than her fatigue. Sister came back with another suggestion: perhaps Father could drive the girl and messenger home. I couldn't, the jeep was laid up. She still had another: maybe the girl's father wasn't desperately sick. I couldn't take that chance and keep his child. Finally, the good sister knocked me over the head with an aside whisper, the Zulu equivalent for: "Father, for heaven's sake, wise up! This guy wants the girl for himself; the old man is not sick at all." She, being a native, knew the native mind. In five minutes I had the gallant gent on his way. Sister, eyes down demurely, calmly continued her basket weaving with the rescued girl at her side. Her thoughts: "How simple can you get! The young priests they send us nowadays!"

All nuns are unsung heroes, but native girls who respond to the call are often heroic before they even become nuns. Take the young girl who came to the mission one day. She was fully grown and not homely. Her scant clothes were old and torn, she was dreadfully dirty, there were long scratches on her arms and legs. It was a penetrating cold day, and she was shivering. Hunger hung in her black eyes. Her face was drawn and nervous; she had a desperate, hunted look.

She had run away from home three days before and had been living in the forest like an animal so as not to be seen. Not a gentle forest either, but dense bush where no native lived. She came from a large pagan family, had attended our school, and decided to become a nun in this Native Congregation of Servite Sisters. It was fine until she became marriageable; then her father and brothers had different designs. She could bring in ten or fifteen head of cattle from a prospective husband. These cattle could in turn be used for another wife for the father or one of the brothers. The market is plentiful, and down here, every "Barkus is willin'." You can't blame the family for their view. It's been there for centuries; they know no better.

The girl's courage was out of this world. They locked her in a hut and told her to drop this fantastic idea of not taking a husband. What do white people know about these things? They starved her, beat her, and even put a few young men in the hut with her at night. She ran away several times. The day we saw her straggling into the mission was one. Finally the family gave up. She went to the novitiate, and a few years ago made her profession in the presence of her family. She's now a young teaching sister in our school. Her story is similar to that of many of the forty or fifty African Servite nuns.

A mission is really not a full-fledged mission without the good sisters. I know, I struggled on missions lacking them: Star of the Sea and Good Shepherd — although at the present time Good Shepherd has a group of our Servite African Sisters. Without the help of the sisters the poor padre is never untroubled. On Saturday morning, for instance, a time for paying the servants and workers and for doing Sunday's chores, he finds himself checking the cleaning, sleuthing for some missing food, counting heads in the catechism class, arranging Sunday vestments. With sisters he can be gloriously free of all this and can settle down to tending to some strictly priestly business.

The African sisters have a gentle and effective way of raising the tone of the mission. After all, a mission is not an ordinary place. But the pagans around us do not realize that. White priests and brothers are an unknown quantity: we don't sell bread and we don't lock them up. The presence of the sisters, however, lets them know something of the purpose of the mission. A drunken native might come singing and dancing down the road and inadvertently prance onto the grounds. Happily he hops around, lord of all he surveys, until he spots Sister in the garden. She slowly straightens up and looks at him. It's enough to tell him he's in the wrong place. He quiets down, and slinks off, until he is far enough away from the mission to comfortably whoop it up again.

With the children the sisters perform miracles. At our High Mass on Sunday morning, sitting down for the Credo, I can't resist watching the small kids in the front pews. Cute little shiny black faces peeking over the top of the kneeler with wide white grins at me; their tiny mouths, big lips and all, laboring over the difficult Latin syllables. Imagine! Yesterday they were in the bush climbing trees in monkey skins. Today they're in bright pinafores singing the Gregorian Chant of the Mass! Who's the magician? Sister Mary Somebody-or-other.

Every morning after Mass our priest house is swarming with little girls doing the housework. Sister attacks with her crew and in no time the place is sparkling. It may not seem like much until you consider that these same kids (and Sister, too, not long before) never saw a bed, a desk, an easy chair, a kitchen sink, until they were introduced to ours by the sister. Now, still in awe at white people's things, they do a slow but excellent job. You are liable to come back into your room after breakfast and find a little tyke under the desk rubbing at an ink spot. She'd work there all day unless you reminded her it was time for school.

Teaching the children these little things, along with catechism, takes the infinite patience and ineffable finesse that our native sisters have. Certainly we priests don't have it. I took in two little boys and tried to teach them the mysteries of making a bed and sweeping a room clean. It was fine until they did their first solo. That night I got into bed and almost broke my leg; they had French-sheeted me. I plunged a foot through the folded sheet, and vowed to beg the Bishop for sisters.

They're half pastors too, these barefooted wonder-workers. Not that they ever infringe on the priest's realm. The opposite is true on that score — they take orders from me "like I was the pope," even on things native, which they know far better. They are semipastors in the sense that the people find it easier to come to them for their wants. All day long there are two or three old cronies hanging around the sisters' convent, pagan and Catholic alike. They chatter with the sisters, often help them with their work, sewing or washing, and the result is that Sister is in close contact with the local gossip. If anything in my line turns up, she's at my door in a minute.

I was tempted to say that Sister would flutter over to me and tell it in a breathless whisper and expanded details. But you don't get that from the native sisters. They never get excited, no matter how serious the matter is. That calm native nature keeps them balanced and levelheaded. They never get ulcers. They never soar pietistical heights. They live close to the earth and close to their people. And in Africa the earth is earthy and so are the people!

As must be rather obvious by now, another black right arm for the white missionary besides the native sisters is the catechist. Inestimable is the value of a good catechist. It is he who has the thankless job of clearing rubble and rocks from the field so the priest can come along and plow. Without him we are almost helpless in a virgin area. The catechist must introduce us, knock down prejudice against us, and do maintenance work on the seedlings of Catholicism.

They come and go, catechists do, and the best one who ever came and went from us was a man named Baldwin Memela. Where he got that first name God knows, but the surname, Memela, is deep Zulu stock. By comparison with other specimens of catechists we knew, Memela was good. One fellow we had visited beer kraals only, styled himself an apostle to drunks. His disciples carried him home once too often, and he found himself out of a job. Another used to water down the Mass wine. Another had an appetite for American paper money (which occasionally comes our way), went off with some, tried to use it in Durban, and ended up breaking rocks.

Catechists are not easy to get, because there are so few. They are obtained by writing to other missions, inquiring from priests, bishops, higher schools. We came upon Memela by pure coincidence, a conversation over a cup of tea with a native who knew him. I leaped at the opportunity, wrote a letter, and soon he was on the mission ready for work.

Memela was no ordinary native, no ordinary Catholic. He was forty-two years old, born of Catholic parents, married to

one Catholic wife, and had five grown children. He was proud
of his Zulu ancestry. He had been around far more than most
native men: a policeman, a soldier overseas during World War
II, a truck driver in Johannesburg, a day laborer, a teacher —
but most of all a catechist. That was the job he liked best and
wanted to keep till death.

I took him on to help open a new school. His worth showed
immediately. We visited the local chief's kraal on a day they
were having a feast. I was hesitant to enter the great yard filled
with hundreds of rough native celebrators; they didn't know
me, some had been drinking, and just the large wild crowd made
me timid. Memela saw it, and in his inimitable unobstrusive
manner took over. Before I had time to lose courage and tell him
we'd come back another day, he respectfully advised that this
would be an excellent opportunity for them to see their new
missionary. Then he quietly waited for my decision. I gulped and
told him to lead on.

Inside the yard, groups of young men and women were dancing grotesquely, waving sticks and spears; other were hustling
beer pots; kids were chasing goats and dogs. And into this
bedlam came a young white priest in short pants accompanied
by his tall catechist. Suddenly the whole yard caught sight of
us and stopped dead. Four or five hundred black faces studied
the two of us. Memela, head high, looked them over calmly; I
watched him not knowing what to do. Quietly he called a ter-
rified woman over and asked her to get a stump for me and
place it next to the chief. Recognizing a command, the woman
scampered and returned immediately with the stump. They
were wide-eyed as Memela led me over to the chief and with
suave dignity made the necessary introductions. I watched him
and knew I had a real catechist. There was no bowing or scraping, as with other catechists I have had. Yet he oozed manly respect for the chief. In three or four clear Zulu sentences he told
the chief my position and purpose among his people. He
laughed and talked easily with the chief, bringing me into the

conversation comfortably. The chief and I were friendly as Memela slipped into the background. It may not sound like much, but going between black and white, especially in matters of religion, takes the utmost skill.

He had a way of quickly sizing up any situation, Memela, an extremely useful quality for a catechist. We were squatted around a huge fire late one afternoon at a kraal near an outstation. The headman of the kraal had killed a goat and invited some friends to the roasting. The first wife of the kraal presented us with two nice cuts. She knelt before us and placed the sizzling meat on a wooden platter. Suddenly there was a sharp, agonizing scream ten feet away from me. It came from an old woman. I looked up and saw the headman cruelly beating the bony hands of this old woman; the heavy stick made dull thuds. Memela saw me grimace and motioned to me not to move. The old woman had grabbed a piece of meat without permission. The beating stopped when the blood oozed from her hands and forearms. I watched her pull the wrapping from her long flat breasts and fold her throbbing hands into it like a muff.

The meat looked good, but my appetite was gone after that episode. The old woman just sat there sobbing quietly. I asked Memela in English, "Should I reprimand the headman? He likes me and may listen." In a minute Memela had a solution and I followed it. On his advice I called the man over; he was calm now, acting as if he just swatted a fly. I asked him for the use of his knife. He cleaned it and handed it to me with a smile; I sliced off a large hunk of the meat he had given me, handed it to Memela and, in clear loud Zulu, told Memela to present it to the old woman crying next to us. Then I politely handed the knife back to the headman. He got the point. Fifteen minutes later he was over giving another chunk of meat to the woman and they were all made up, laughing together.

A priest necessarily spends a lot of time with his catechist, often days together. And under the difficult living conditions at an outstation or on a tent trip, the catechist can easily be bothersome. Not Memela. He was excellent company. Had a quick wit — native style of course — could always make me laugh with his mimics and imitations. He could do a take-off on any of our priests and brothers perfectly, and knew well all my own idiosyncrasies.

Often on our visits the people would offer us native beer. Neither of us objected to the drink. It's not scotch and soda, but on a hot afternoon in the sweltering bush you're not particular. Being home brew, this native beer has a different strength and quality at each kraal. Memela and I had little respect for the watery stuff, but we had to be polite. He would sip it first, and if it was good and had a kick, he'd say in Zulu as he took the pot away from his lips, "The battery is charged." If it was weak, "The battery is flat." Our hosts never knew. They thought we were talking about the jeep. After quaffing a few charged batteries this became a huge joke between us.

Memela had a serious side, too. Sitting around a fire or squatting under a tree eating lunch, we would have long conversations; he could talk naturally and sincerely about the great efforts missionaries were making to lift up his backward people. He asked sensible and deep questions about the Faith, about the Church's beginnings, about the life of Christ, and about the Mass.

Proof of this interest in the Mass was brought home vividly to me one day. We had set up a monthly Mass at a new kraal. The attendance was awful, and after five months it was worse. The few who came were pagans, who had no respect for anything. They kidded about worshiping God, boasted of being friends of Satan, liked only things like beer, sassy girls, and Mambo. They laughed outright during the Canon and never listened to the sermon; I had corrected them several times and was losing patience and becoming discouraged. Finally, the day came when, after a dreadful ride, a long fast, a flat tire, I arrived and found no one there. I said Mass alone with Memela, had a sandwich breakfast, and waited for them. When they showed, I blasted them for not appreciating the worship of God, and told them I would not have Mass at their place any more. They couldn't care less.

All the way home Memela was quiet — respectful, polite, but unusually quiet. Later in the day while I was taking it easy on the cool veranda he came over and began talking slowly about his days in the catechist's school and all the wonderful things he had learned there about our Faith. Half-interested I nodded and made the necessary grunts (Zulu is full of grunts). Casually he asked me if it was really true, all this about the great value of the Mass; it seemed he remembered something along that line, but wasn't sure. Ever primed, I took off immediately on the infinite merits of the Mass, the great blessings for those present. . . . He just kept looking at me, strangely, patiently, wisely. It rang a bell. Next month we were back at that kraal and in the midst of its din was the Mass. I can't report that the pagans flocked to us there, but our perseverance did bring home to them the sincerity and seriousness of our work. No white man, they thought, would take such a rebuff from natives and come back for more unless he had something worthwhile. And we knew we had that in the Mass. We figured to let it work on their hardness, their ignorance, their indifference in its own mysterious way. Mass is still being celebrated in that hut, and is now looked forward to.

Not only was Memela a capable catechist, but he had great missionary zeal. You pay regular wages to a catechist, above those of the common laborer and below those of a schoolteacher. He earns this money if he simply goes around, with or without the priest, and invites the surrounding natives to church. But our Memela did more than invite; he urged, cajoled, threatened. Out-and-out pagans were putty in his hands as his well-trained tongue punched holes in their best excuses for not coming to worship God. And they learned to like it.

Once we ran into a fairly prosperous-looking native "gentleman." He had on white man's clothes, dirty and clumsily worn, however; and a table and chair in his hut. He greeted us with a big breezy American hello instead of the slow phlegmatic proper Zulu greeting. He was quick to inform us that he, too, was a member of the cloth. Not only had he found the true church, but he had founded it. That thatch hut on the hill was it!

Memela ached to get at him. We parked ourselves in his hut, got through the preliminaries in a hurry, and then they went at it. Crackling Zulu flashed back and forth. The "gentleman" threw at Memela all the hackneyed stuff he knew, spiced it with dramatic gestures and emphasis. Memela came right back at him with some of his own corn. Talk about colored preachin' men on Lake Street! They twisted and turned Scripture to mean anything they pleased, and then rounded off with clamoring curlicues. Before I left I asked the man if he would like to visit us some Sunday for Mass. Yes, if I would let him preach. The "preacher" in turn invited me to his church. I answered that I would think about it, but later Memela told me I should not go because he would capitalize on it by telling his people that even the white Umfundisi worships at his great church. I never went to him and he never came to us.

Another time we walked unsuspectingly into a lunatic's kraal. The yard was unkempt, paths were all weeds, debris everywhere. The occupant was alone at his small fire inside the broken-down hut. We entered and squatted on the dirty floor. He had a queer look about him, and seemed to be speaking nothing but gibberish. When the fellow reached around for a bit of snuff lying in the corner, Memela motioned to me that he was "mental."

It would be against custom to leave immediately, so we lingered. I looked around the hut, saw the usual large bush knife lying next to him. My imagination jumped to what he could do with that if the notion to use it came into his strange head. Also there were spears stuck in the thatch of the roof. I wasn't for hanging around long. Memela babbled on with him for a while, then smoothly explained that we had to leave. Our host didn't like it, but he didn't reach for his knife or spears, just leered crazily at us as we ducked through the entrance into the fresh air.

Soon after that our good Memela died. He caught cerebral malaria, a dreadful disease, not rare here, that snuffs out life in a matter of hours. Some mosquito at our newest outstation, Kwambuzi, injected him with the germ that put an end to a great catechist and a great native helper. He received the last rites a few minutes before he lost his mind and life.

The announcement of the visit of a native bishop was received with surprising indifference. It was not easy, spreading the word about the coming of the Church's first and only Zulu bishop to our Ingwavuma mission. Our people's idea of a priest is still vague; now we were asking them to swallow this new term, "bishop," and choking them by adding "native." For weeks I visited huts and tried to get over to them what a great privilege it is for the mission to have such a distinguished visitor, and how they should not miss seeing him.

The idea was just too massive for them. I had thought the announcement would knock them off their grass mats, but their reaction was lukewarm. "He's one of your own!" I told them. "Surnamed Dlamini, the very name of your chief! Don't you catch on, man, this thing is great, an enormous stride for the Church and your people!" It would have been easier to explain the Chicago Loop. The small circle of people sitting around the hut stared at me with blank faces. One asked, "This Zulu man, who is what you call a bishop, does he have a wife?" "Of course not," I answered impatiently. Then they came to life as I thought they should have before. All began to jabber. Some burst out laughing, others made wise cracks I couldn't catch but could guess at. Sure, they would come to see this black bishop, en masse, rain or shine: "A Zulu man without a wife, this we gotta see!"

The idea of the visit was to show the bishop our backward area, and also spark any dormant native vocations. At least, the sight of a native clergyman and bishop would give the people a general idea of what we white missionaries are eventually after down here. The native sisters and catechists help greatly, but native priests will be the backbone of the future African Church. Thus far, we have only one native Servite priest teaching in Swaziland, Father Albert Ndebele, a young, recently ordained Zulu who is now doing advanced studies in Canon Law in Rome. Perhaps the splash of the visit of a native bishop might start a few more vocations among our little rascals.

And it was definitely a splash, Bishop Dlamini's visit. He arrived on a bright sunny afternoon accompanied by our own Servite bishop, Rt. Rev. Barneschi. As he stepped out of the car, the school children, sisters, teachers, and many passers-by looked on. You could almost hear the united gasp from them as they watched us priests and brothers greet both bishops. Down we went on one knee and kissed each ring with equal respect — a rare sight indeed in South Africa. It was only the beginning of the surprises. I took Bishop Dlamini's traveling bag from his hand, stepped aside and motioned him through the door first. A quick glance over to the crowd showed me they hadn't missed a thing. That was what we wanted. They, in turn, would go home and tell others about the strange things taking place at the Roman Mission. They would gossip and rehash it in their endless gab around fires, and maybe a drop or two of our Catholicity would stick.

That evening before supper we young missionaries — four still studying Zulu — priest and brothers, listened to the veterans. The room was filled with the pleasant chink of ice in glass, tall, frosted, cool-looking things that are so highly appreciated in tropical climates. But the conversation was nothing like that of a cocktail bar. South Africa is a country in ferment. Catholics and their leaders, bishops and priests, are girding themselves for the worst — which, from all the signs, is coming. The bishops told us of their quickly summoned conferences, their interviews with government officials, their future plans as the thinly veiled booms are lowered on Church activity, especially in our schools. Bishop Dlamini's high-pitched voice had no fear in it, yet his was a fearfully tense position. Bishop Barneschi spoke of the coming turmoil with calmness as cool as the Tom Collins in his episcopal hand. Bishop and missionary for so many years, he was accustomed to storms. Yet even he admitted that racial winds in South Africa had never before been so menacing.

We paid close attention to the bishops, but I found myself concentrating more on the native bishop than our own. I stared at the man, hard, almost impolitely; pictured him as a boy, like the many boys I see all day, monkey skins around their loins, running in the veld, climbing trees, herding cattle, chasing lizards — semiwild. Hardly an apt environment for the rearing of a future bishop! Yet it was true, he had been a herdboy and now he had a sparkling pectoral cross hanging where his little slingshot had once been.

Rt. Rev. Bishop Bonaventure Dlamini, F.F.J., was born about the year 1905. With natives you can seldom learn the exact date of birth. The closest you can get is something like, "before the big storm," "after that great famine," "the year of the big bush fire." He was the son of a minor chief who had ruled a district some hundred miles south and west of Durban — the area of the present Mayertown. His surname, Dlamini, is indicative of royal Zulu blood. When natives give that surname as their own they do so with a slight erectness and proud tilt of their heads. His parents were pagan and unschooled. A chief, even a minor one, cannot well afford to become a Christian and have only one wife. He would not be respected or obeyed and would soon lose his rule.

Yet the future bishop's father was not opposed to the nearby Catholic missionaries who were located at a mission called Mariatal. The boy frequently wandered around the mission, watched the brothers grind corn, build, work the farm. Occasionally he would score with a piece of bread or candy from one of the priests. He was fascinated by those white men in long robes who were always moving about on their horses and who usually made him and his little friends laugh.

Eventually he persuaded his father to permit him to stay at the mission and attend school. Once he had left his kraal he never returned except to visit. He grew up on Mariatal Mission, remained there year after year until he entered the newly erected St. Mary's Seminary for native vocations at Ixopo, a town just south of Pietermaritzburg.

He was ordained on November 28, 1937, the second priest from there and the first religious priest to be ordained from St. Mary's. He had joined the congregation called Franciscan Familiars of St. Joseph. That is what the F.F.J. stands for after his name.

The Catholic Church as well as the growing number of native Catholics of Zululand were aching for native priests, and Father Dlamini responded, burning with priestly zeal. For years he was assistant parish priest at various missions under the care of the Mariannhill Fathers. He was a go-between, helped the white pastors to understand his people, and helped his people to understand the work of the Church. Actually, he was somewhat of a test case of native priests, and he knew it, and shouldered the responsibility accordingly.

He was made pastor of St. Boniface Mission and he ran it with care and prudence. Later he was assigned to take over the St. Magdalene Mission, where he was also a successful and understanding pastor. Rome itself had her wise old eyes on him for episcopal timber, and on February 21, 1954, the appointment was made. Archbishop Damiano was the Apostolic Delegate and it was through him that the Church took this bold and courageous step forward. On April 26, 1954, he was consecrated at Lourdes Cathedral as Diocesan Bishop of Umzimkulu. This diocese is located south and west of Durban and was established in 1954, being separated from the Diocese of Mariannhill.

It comprises the civil districts of Umzimkulu, Harding, Port Shepstone, Bulwer, and Himeville. Bishop Dlamini had come a long way and had gigantic responsibility.

Our small chapel would not hold all the natives we were sure would come to the pontifical Mass scheduled for 10 o'clock in the morning; so we built an outside altar on the front veranda. Catholic, Protestant, and pagan were warmly invited. Our big truck brought in the catechumens from the outstations. At nine o'clock little groups were already squatting in the front yard. While we waited for the last load from the farthest outstation, Bishop Dlamini asked me to bring him out to the people. All eyes turned on him as he walked out the door, tall, thin, and impressive in his red flowing robes. As we came to the first group I made some remark to them that usually got a laugh. They didn't even know I was there. Their eyes were glued to the bishop, wide, staring, studying every inch of him. He was used to such looks, used to native ways. He paused before greeting them, then went into the weather and their burnt crops, and got a few of their surnames. It was elegantly smooth. Catholic and pagan alike were at ease with him, laughing naturally and talking quietly. I thought of how right the pope was in his advice about native clergy having the jump on us with their people. He went from one to another unhurriedly, giving them all a good long look.

The Mass impressed the backwoods natives and deeply pleased the few Catholics we have. What a sight it was for them: a native going through those solemn ceremonies with us white priests buzzing around the altar assisting! Here was the Catholicity they had learned about in the catechism right before their eyes. Our Church practiced what it preached.

But most of all perhaps the natives remember the sermon of Bishop Dlamini. They're great talkers, these slow-moving natives. They are gifted with natural eloquence and are not embarrassed on their feet. Here was a native, priest and bishop, giving forth Catholic doctrine as natives had never heard it before. He began slowly and quietly; no one bowls over native mentality — one works at it gently. In two minutes they were spellbound, and perfectly silent.

"You want to be as happy as fish swimming in the water? Then worship God properly!" Every thought was laced with rich Zulu idioms. They don't sound like much to us, but they hit home with the natives. The speaker's voice went up and down while his tongue clicked out the Zulu sounds; he paced, but not enough to distract from what he was saying. At times he got angry and blasted, spitting the words out: "You parents refuse to send your children to school, yet you send your cattle to the dipping tanks. God will treat you too as cattle!" He urged them to lift themselves up, to co-operate with the mission. He went even so far as to say he himself, at one time, was more ignorant than they; he too had "old eyes," — meaning pagan thoughts; as the Church had lifted him, it could also lift them and their children.

It was a sermon that is still ringing in the huts of Ingwavuma. The following day we didn't have boys and girls flocking to us to become priests and sisters; no, but there must have been a few thinking about it. Perhaps their children, one or two among Ingwavuma's thousands, will join the ranks of our black helpers. Africa, the natives, the Church Herself, move slowly.

6. White Helpers

THE pope's advice, the Church's policy, as has been said, is to aim at establishing a native clergy in Africa. It's that ancient, Roman, long-range view. And it will come about some day. But meanwhile, we white missionaries must care for the infant Church in Africa. It might be a hundred, two hundred years, before the toddling baby becomes a man and manages for himself. We won't leave him too early; even in his terrible teens, the white missionaries will still need to assist the African Church.

And right now, at least in our backward area of Zululand, the black baby Church hasn't even begun to crawl. Why, we're still at the four-hour feeding stage, broken sleep at night, no rest during the day, cleaning up, always bustling around. It's rewarding and rich even in human comforts, this ceaseless care for our infant black Catholicism — who doesn't enjoy caring for the children they love? And in our job we are not alone. There is another type of missionary besides the priest and sister who helps, a missionary whose lot in life is very humble, seldom publicized, often unappreciated, and always hard. He is the missionary lay brother.

A lay brother is one who joins the Order to assist in the good works of the Order by his manual labor. He is a full-fledged religious; that is, he has been trained in our novitiate, has taken the three vows of poverty, chastity, and obedience, and is bound to our Rule. His difficult vocation of humility and obedience is invaluable on the missions. Down here the brother is more than a handy man, more than a jack-of-all-trades, more than a convenient cog in monastic machinery. The missionary brother does everything but celebrate Mass and hear confessions. He plans buildings, draws blueprints, cuts roads; he cares for boarding children, handles some administration, governs workers; takes care of the sick, makes coffins, digs graves. And he prays.

One of the best of our missionary brothers is a man named Timothy Culhane. When he was transferred back to America, Africa suffered a loss. I'll never forget seeing him off at the docks in Durban. The huge passenger ship nestled close to the pier, her newly-painted, bright white superstructure glaring blindingly in the hot African sun. Black burly bodies of half-clad native workmen swarmed over her like hordes of anxious ants. Massive cranes trundled up and stretched long steel arms into her bowels. Water belched from her side drains and splashed in the dirty harbor. You looked at it and thought of faraway places. High on her proud prow the name stood out in bold black letters: AFRICA. And high on the narrow gangplank Tim waved good-by to us and his dear Africa.

He, together with our late Father Michael Delehanty, planted the Star of the Sea Mission in that extremely difficult Thongoland area. In spite of the claims of our novices in Granville, Wisconsin, Thongoland *is* the end of the world, not Granville. Even these hardy South African whites sit up and listen when we talk about that country, because talk is as close as the majority get to Thongoland. Malaria is more rampant there than anywhere in the Union. It's fiercely hot. There are no roads, just sand paths. But, thanks to the sweat of Brother Tim, Father Mike, and others, a thriving mission is there.

At Star of the Sea during their first six months Father Delehanty and Tim had to live in a tent. Tim built the present large school from the ground up. He began by making concrete blocks on the site. Cement had to be hauled from the nearest railhead, eighty-five miles away. After working all day, either driving the big truck or driving native workers, Tim would come back to the tent, rustle up some supper, remove all the debris from his stretcher bed and flop down exhausted. Father Delehanty was tired too because, while Tim was building, Mike was out visiting natives, getting acquainted. In the morning, the debris was shifted from the center of the tent back to the bed to make room for the portable altar and Father Delehanty's Mass. So it went until the shell of the house and school were up. And they went up simultaneously. Father Mike and Tim did not put their own comfort before that essential mission item, the school.

Breakdown stories are Tim's by the dozen. The big truck seemed to be jinxed: it's not improbable either that Satan and his powerful crowd could not have been happy about a mission sprouting in their Thongoland stronghold. Things happened to the GMC that General Motors never heard of. It was nothing to be riding along and have the left rear wheel come rolling by the cab seconds before the heavy load crashed down on the exposed axle.

The Ubombo Mountain lies between Star of the Sea and the rail station; climbing up and down it you need brakes, good ones. Not once, but many times, the truck's brakes gave out without the slightest warning, and for seemingly no reason. On one trip from the station, as Tim, with a load of four tons of cement, was approaching the first curve of the long, fast-dropping road leading down, he braked to shift into a lower gear. The pedal slammed to the floor, useless. Four tons of cement behind and a two thousand foot drop in elevation looming up ahead! The heavy truck quietly began to roll, picking up speed. Tim turned off the engine, told the helper to hold tight, then cut the wheels hard and rolled the truck over on its back just before reaching the steep downgrade. The truck lay upside down, wheels spinning as he and the helper climbed out with a few minor scratches.

Building was Tim's primary work, but on the missions no

The author recruiting for school children

Brother Tim and workers at Star of the Sea

Ingwavuma. Typical kraal scene. Woman is first wife and a catechumen.

Star of the Sea area. The author baptising an old woman.

Tent Mass

Matchamhlope outstation

Pagan women visit crib beneath altar in Ingwavuma Mission chapel.

Chapel at Good Shepherd Mission, Hiabisa

Strictly for
the grandstands

A seasoned Zulu warrior who means
business — if his right cross misses,
his left jab won't. He holds a
knobkerry in his right hand,

Bottle race at Ingwavuma football field behind priest's house

Father Delahanty exploring Maputa area before founding of Star of the Sea Mission

Day of profession of perpetual vows — African Servite Sisters

Sister Theresa teaching catechism

Brother Tim
poses with
Nora, Star of
the Sea, Maputa.

Star of the Sea Mission,
1953. Brother Tim's workers
carrying the bell-tower post
to position. They are
singing a lifting song.

Red at a quiet moment

Brother Jack's Kwambuzi school finished

One of the oldest catechists, trained by Benedictine Fathers,
Augustine Zitha, an intelligent, dedicated worker.

They just saw their first white man.

Baby-
sitting

Off for supplies to Gollel Rail Station — Miles of sheer
delight for the altar boys in back

Father General at Maputa reception

Fathers Taucci, General, and Ortmann crossing
Pongola River on Nkuzzi-bomvu's barge

Old Land Rover, young Servite (the Umfundisi), and Zulu warriors pondering sermon just preached on this one-wife, white-man nonsense.

Father Kinch and Sister Annunciata pose with First Communion class at Ingwavuma.

The congregation after a kraal Mass pose in their finery with the Umfundisi.

Chief Balekelwe (left) with his man in attendance facing a group of tribal consultors outside his hut, Ingwavuma

The Umfundisi and the warrior

Star of the Sea Mission. Brother Tim directing working crew in making firmer roadbed through stream. Native with black hat is Ignatius Nzalo, our catechist.

Zulu warrior twins

one has an exclusive job; we're all missionaries, period. And missionaries are ad-libers to the core. Father takes the jeep out on Saturday and is due back in the afternoon. The jeep breaks down and Father doesn't get home until Sunday afternoon. Meanwhile our catechumens arrive on Sunday morning for Mass. Brother Tim steps in and holds the fort, leading the rosary, singing hymns, kidding the children about their catechism mistakes, and sympathizing with the aches and pains of the old people. All the time his eyes are on the road, sweating it out for the priest.

He could not administer all the sacraments, but Brother Tim has lined up many a lucky native for baptism by the priest. While mixing cement with his workers, he would overhear their talk about some sick old man ready to die. He would get the details: where the man is, how to travel there, and if no priest was available at the time he would go out himself with the catechist. Some of these hardheaded old pagans want no part of baptism, but others agree to it, and cash in at the last moment. So keen was Tim on this that it became common for the natives to let him know when anyone around the mission was near death. They always knew something would be done, and fast, whether a trip to the hospital or a trip to the priest. Many times Tim got there late, but even then, he helped dig the grave or shook hands with the mourning relatives.

Everybody on the mission is, of course, important — the priests, sisters, teachers, servants. Each has his job. But take away the brother for a few days and you can almost watch the mission crumble. Father Delehanty and I had a session of it when Tim was gone for a while. It was during that year I was stationed at Star of the Sea with them. We got up one morning and found that there was no water and no light. Father Delehanty took his flashlight and went down to work on the water pump; I took my light out to the generator. We must have made a sight, two sleepy-eyed mechanics who could hardly name the tools. The engines no doubt knew we were a couple of phonies;

they had that confident, contrary look about them that seemed
to say: "We'll bow to Tim, a worthy opponent, but no giving
in to you two characters!" And they didn't. Half hour later when
Mike and I met at the house, his shirt was torn, hands and
face full of grease and sand, and no water coming up. I had
stubbed my toes, broken my flashlight, and the only electricity
I got was a resounding shock that landed me in a thorn bush.
Tim came home a few days later and both engines practically
started up themselves.

They grew to know and love Tim, the natives of Thongoland,
just as they do all our good brothers. Proof of that was the
send-off they had for him, the biggest thing ever seen at Star
of the Sea. Hordes of natives came from miles around. Our
hundreds of school children, including those from the three outschools, many of whom he had encouraged personally (and
sometimes dragged) to school; old men and women whom he
had helped get the government old age pension by piling them
on the truck and driving them to see the Magistrate. In order
to get the pension it is necessary to appear in person, and because of the distance and their age, that was impossible until
Tim came along. All his workers were there. These knew him
best; they admired his ability, respected his orders, and feared
that menacing look. Everybody was warm in their display of
affection that day.

One who felt Tim's leaving most at Star of the Sea was a
little native girl named Nora. She was about six years old, an
orphan or castaway, with clean even teeth, beautiful black
flashing eyes, and a pretty dimpled face full of cute twists. A
real charmer who had been at the mission for three years. She
idolized "Blata Tim." When word got around that he was
leaving, she was quiet for days and then solemnly asked if
she could go to his home with him across the water. The
other kids laughed, and Tim went along with the joke telling her she could if she got a suitcase to pack her things in.
On the day of Tim's leaving, Nora was seen hurrying every-

where, looking frantically in the sheds, under the house, around the school. So busy was she that she did not line up for candy with the other kids.

In the late afternoon Tim got his luggage into the jeep and was pumping gas for the trip to Ingwavuma. Hundreds of natives were standing around making noise and last jokes with Tim. Nora ran up sweating and out of breath, excited eyes dancing. On top of her head was balanced an old cardboard box, bulging and tied with native twine. She was ready.

Poor Tim saw his mistake, and so did the people around. The noise stopped. Tim turned away, fussed with the gas pump, fussed with his suitcases, and finally faced Nora. He bent down to her slowly, took her tiny shoulders in his rough hands, looked at her for a long time, then said simply, "Nora, you cannot come with me. I must go home alone." She stared at him unbelieving for a second, then shuddered slightly. Slowly she took the box of clothes off her head, put it down on the sand, sat on it, put her pretty head into her tiny hands, and wept quietly.

The main task of the missionary brother is twofold: he must build new buildings, and maintain the old. Both jobs are absorbing time consumers. Fortunately, labor here is cheap and plentiful. But Brother's helpers can give him many a gray hair. They're just raw natives, clever with twigs and thatch and a bush knife, but dense when it comes to building white-man's houses of bricks and steel. They must be constantly watched and corrected.

With our terrible shortage of brothers the ones here must have a dozen arms to keep up. And the way some of them work you would think they had. Our young, noisy Brother Jack LeMay from Detroit is a good example. When he was stationed at Good Shepherd I tagged along with him one day. After Mass and breakfast he went out to boss a gang of twelve native laborers who were putting up an additional wall to the priest house. (These native men, by the way, earn about $10 month; work six days a week.) He fired Zulu at them fast and sure, let them know he wanted no monkey business on this job. Then he clearly showed them, especially the two bricklayers, what to do; drew lines and diagrams so even the most stupid caught on.

By the time he had that gang started the cook had put a good-sized lunch into the truck, and Jack was off to do some repairing at an outschool. Nothing much — just a roof caved in. He fixed that and was back in the afternoon and up on the wall with his main gang. While there, a boy came over to say there was a leak in the water tank. It was an understatement, the pipe had broken right off — some kid had tried to chin himself on it. There was no calling up to have a man come out, no picking up a new pipe at the corner hardware. Jack warmed the blowtorch, got some other tools, and had the tank in working order before supper.

Our model outschool at Ndumu — in an outstation of Ingwavuma — was Jack's first major project. This Ndumu area is located just south of the Portuguese East African border, about forty miles from the Ingwavuma Mission. One of the Servite Fathers' best white South African friends, a storekeeper named Roy Rutherford, was instrumental in obtaining two acres of land there. Such friendly gestures to us missionaries are very rare indeed, and we were deeply grateful to him for the Ndumu site. It is in deep bush country, the middle of nowhere, but well populated with natives who had never heard of the Roman Catholic Church. The first day Jack loaded his work shack onto the big truck, whistled the laborers aboard and was on his way. That day his most important tool was the familiar bush knife. With unbounded enthusiasm and a strong right arm Jack cleared space enough to move around in The local natives stood agape wondering what this friendly grinning whiteman would do next. Their eyes popped a few hours later when they saw his shack set up, stove and bed and groceries arranged neatly.

Brother Jack has a unique way of kidding the natives. On

that first day at the Ndumu site one happened to ask him if he was going to build a hospital. That was all. Jack took off with gestures and ringing Zulu describing how he intended to build another Johns-Hopkins. It would stretch from here to that far hill over there. He would fill it with pills and pillows and no one would be sick anymore, thanks to the Roman Catholics. When they caught on, a loud guffaw went up and they seemed amazed that a white man could tell a joke. Some slower ones didn't laugh at all, just stared at Jack and asked when the huge hospital would open.

Cement is bought and carried to the place, but sand and water for making blocks have to be found in the area, or hauling bills become excessive. It meant for Jack, cutting new roads to the nearest water hole, filling large gasoline drums with water, and carting these back to the site. The same with sand. No one is around to advise him where these places are or how to get to them. No one tells him anything; he's on his own as he never was before. There are hurdles every day: like the time one of his key laborers took a fit right on the job. Jack got scared but not as much as the other workers. They were all going to run off immediately, suspecting that they were jinxed by this white man. A few quickly-produced shillings convinced them otherwise.

Jack is no slowpoke, as other white builders in the area will verify; they are constantly amazed at his speed and thoroughness. He squared off the foundations at Ndumu and was pouring cement into them within a month. That's record time for bush country. His organization and treatment of the workers were on a friendly basis but effective. They liked him and his carefree ways, but they produced for him too. When he would return to the main mission at Ingwavuma after four or five days of work at Ndumu we would ask him how high the walls were now; it was only a few months before he was pointing far over his head.

After six months at the Ndumu site the walls were up and

Jack was tackling the complicated roofing problems. This is when the natives began to take notice and nose around the building. Wandering, wild little kids for the most part, but all possibles for the school. A kind word from Jack, now especially, might mean a pupil next year; an angry look when a beam didn't fit or the sun was hot might mean frightening off ten kids so that they would want nothing to do with the Catholics. One day when I was visiting the scene of his work I saw him open a can of beans and instead of pitching the empty can away he set it aside. I wondered. He explained that he was going to give it to the first little guy who happens by. The kids love tin cans. By Divine Grace and such discriminate use of empty tin cans is the Church planted in Africa!

Together with Brother Jack LeMay there is another brother here at the Ingwavuma Mission, Marcel Lavergne, a French Canadian Servite. I think of Marcel often in my work, because a missionary priest is often moving around in one of our various types of vehicles — the jeeps, the car, the trucks. Marcel is the man who keeps these vehicles on the road.

One day I was on a pleasant ride, rolling across the vast African low veld in the late afternoon, returning home after a routine three-dayer at an outstation, looking forward to a clean shower, a few letters, and decent cooking. I was in no hurry: you soon lose your American bustle as slow-moving Africa gets into your blood. Besides, it doesn't pay to go fast on these roads; they're murderous, made of mud, rocks, sand, logs, anything. The open jolting jeep is bearable at ten miles an hour; fifteen and you're hanging on. The sun had been hot, I could tell from the new layer of brown on the back of my hands. An occasional kraal appeared and broke the monotony of scraggly trees and thornbush. It must've been a pleasant ride, because I found myself singing "Only Make Believe . . ." at the top of my Kedzie Avenue voice. "Melancholy Baby," "Harvest Moon," and a few more standbys came after that. It happens inevitably when I'm alone on a long ride. Sorry, but it does.

Strange noises began to come from the engine to spoil my raucous yowling. An innocent scraping that told me nothing because I know nothing about that world of wonders under a hood. The scraping gave way to a second sound, a dull, steady thumping. Singing stopped as I feared a breakdown; it would not be my first. No use stopping because I could never locate the trouble, so foolishly I pushed on. The thumping became a clunking. A sharp screech, a deafening belch from deep in the engine, and the vehicle stopped dead. Sudden silence saturated the jeep and me, nothing to hear but my sighs and the distant forest noises. I got out slowly, took my overnight bag in one hand, the rifle in the other, looked ahead toward the Ingwavuma mountain, and walked. Eight miles uphill.

At home it was an old story and a new job for Brother Marcel Lavergne, who went out and towed the jeep in. What happened was an oil seal had given way, and when the engine oil leaked out, the pistons "froze." I should have noticed the trouble earlier, but book-wise priests do things to vehicles that should not be done to an old shoe. Marcel's mechanical ability is vital in this country, because the vehicle is our life line. Marcel is a meticulous, unhurried, orderly worker whose makeshift shop at the back of the house is a beehive of activity. He has a battery of equipment — grinders, forge, welding outfit, sprayer, tools of all sorts — and he uses it the way a .400 hitter uses his bat.

Our jeep or jeep pickup goes limping into Marcel's shop, a tired, sorry-looking mess, perhaps with a cracked spring, bent frame, leaky valves, worn out shackles, burned-out lights, or a broken crankshaft. A quiet hush comes over Marcel. At such times, he is like a pointer smelling partridge. A few days later the crippled machine is up on stilts, a skeleton. Marcel is nothing if not thorough — every part comes off. Slowly it builds up, going back together with each part cleaned and in perfect working order. Then the day of the trial spin. You can tell it at the breakfast table: Marcel has a peculiar test-pilot ring in his voice as he calls for more eggs. No fear though, there are only minor adjustments to be made, and we have a new vehicle. As it rolls out, another wreck rolls in.

It requires more than mechanical ability, Brother Marcel's job. Ingwavuma, South Africa, is not like America. When you need a new part for your car in Chicago, you just buzz a garage and it's fixed in a matter of hours. Here in the bush you have to be a telephone diplomat, first of all, to get the call through to Durban for the needed spare. It takes hours of gymnastics with crank and receiver box, as well as corny kidding with country bumpkins at the relay stations. The hookup is always weak: the way Marcel shouts on the phone makes me doubt if he needs lines at all for the first twenty miles. Then the operator gets on your back for overtime. To most of us it's maddening. Marcel handles it easily, and often ends with success.

That is, semisuccess. The part may come by train, bus, and runner boy a week or two later, but usually — yes, usually — it's the wrong one. It's phenomenal how confused messages become in this confused country. If you want a rear wheel bearing for the jeep, order a front wheel bushing for the truck and you're in! Marcel puts up with all this as well as he puts up with the hot breaths of the anxious priests waiting for the fixed vehicle. His day is three quarters makeshift: he can't get a new cross member so he welds some steel together and makes one; the spring is oversized, so he cuts it down. And a loose bolt hasn't a chance to remain loose under his practiced hands.

Occasionally one of us priests will be out there watching him work, taking mental notes, and not without reason. Zulu might be our first requisite here, but how to use a spanner runs a close second.

One day I was driving a five-ton load of cement from the rail station back to the home Mission, when the engine conked out. The fuel line often becomes clogged in this sand, and I had been shown how to blow it out. The two native helpers were surprised to see me go to work on the carburetor with screw driver and pliers. My face had the confidence of a Henry Ford, but my head was empty. I huffed and puffed on every hose that had any resemblance to a fuel line, put the carburetor on again, stepped on the starter, and the motor started beautifully. I remember wiping off my hands and nonchalantly explaining to the wide-eyed native boys the principle upon which the carburetor works. Ten minutes later, a mile up the road, she conked out again. The boys slowly handed me tools with the look that only a native can give a boasting white man who has made a fool of himself. They see it often.

With tiny beads of sweat gathering on my forehead I went after the carburetor again. That and the horn were the only two things I could identify under the hood. The horn tooted, so off came the carburetor for another cleaning. It took about twenty minutes. Then I turned the key, and the engine started again.

It was dark now. I was hungry, cranky, and only halfway home. The boys, too, were in no happy mood. Their white-man driver, priest, talker, could not even keep the truck running. They were thinking about their food, fires, and wives at home. During that last stall I had noticed that the flashlight was very weak. Another mile and the truck quit again.

This time not a word was said, and the native helpers did not dare put any kind of a face on. They just handed the tools and hardly breathed. It was easy to see I was becoming desperate. If only I knew what I was doing! Ignorance is what raised my temper because I figured it was some little fault which a mechanic could fix in a minute. I doubted the carburetor, but every time I took it off and put it on, the truck worked for a while.

The boy held the dim flashlight while I dismantled the carburetor again. Soon the light went out completely, and I could hardly see the engine, much less the minute parts of a carburetor. I was finished. I pitched the wrench into the cab, and in the pitch-black silence I leaned against the fender for a weary minute; then I quietly told the boys to climb under the canvas on top of the load and make themselves comfortable for the night. I got in the cab and fell into a deep sleep, exhausted.

In the early morning the hot sun on the steel cab woke me. I sent the boys after Marcel. He arrived just after noon and had the engine running in a matter of minutes. If I had known more about an engine, I too could have repaired it and been home on time the night before. The truck had an automatic choke which was controlled by a thermostat. The setscrew on this temperature apparatus had shaken loose, with the result that when the engine heated, the carburetor flooded and the motor died. Each time while I was taking the carburetor apart and putting it together again the engine would cool and run until it heated up. That's why we watch Marcel whenever we have the chance, to find out about these little adjustments that can keep us moving.

The proper adjustment of a gasoline engine may not seem closely connected to the conversion of African pagans, but it is. Some of our outstations are only visited monthly. If the priest's jeep breaks down, the people don't have Mass. This happens twice and the people begin to think Mass cannot be very important. They don't understand how vehicles break down. All they know is Father didn't come when he said he would. Father's stock drops and with it his Church's.

Opportunities are missed when vehicles quit. A broken-down big truck can delay the completion of an outschool for months. That means months less of catechism classes, months less of contact with the people, maybe a few deathbed baptisms lost. Not that we're typical Americans in a hurry-up scheme to convert Zululand overnight. Africa and conversion move slowly. We understand that well. But opportunities whiz by daily, and often it takes a fast-moving jeep to catch them. Marcel and brothers like him keep our vehicles rolling, and also save face for the less mechanical-minded priests. Thank God for them.

7. Small Fry, Big Catch

NATIVE kids are missionaries' meat. They are the seeds of the Church, the pillars of the parish, little grinning black ragamuffins with running noses and dirty hands. It pays for a missionary to work on them. They are not yet barnacled with paganism, have not been steeped in the superstitions of their elders. They're open-minded, pliable, game for anything — even white-skinned priests with their tall tales about a Man named Jesus.

Here at our budding boarding school of Ingwavuma there are about sixty of them crawling over our backs — forty girls and twenty boys between seven and seventeen — and they tickle. There are all kinds among them: Catholics, pagans, Protestants; good-looking, homely, repulsive; smart, dumb, and two of them are slightly crazy. God created them all, but it would almost seem that we have a few odd ones that even He doesn't know are around. This motley home gang, along with nearly a hundred day pupils, make up our school, and our work. With hesitancy their parents put them under the care of the white people. You can hardly blame them for their reluctance. That boyish-looking priest who came around asking for the kids, why, he could hardly stay on his horse!

Walking bush paths, up and down hills got the best of me, so I decided to buy a horse. His name was Red and he almost got the best of me too. I had never ridden a horse until I got here, and if I'm ever transferred back to America I'll never ride one again. But still the old nag was helpful; he brought me to distant places I could never reach by foot or jeep. I'll have more to say about Red later.

These sixty boarding children depend on us for their any and every want. The native sisters care for them for the most part, but we priests and brothers come in for our share. They even pester the three or four new missionaries learning Zulu, along with the two priests and two brothers assigned to this Ingwavuma Mission. One is always at the door. You hear a faint knock, go out and find a little boy trying not to cry. As soon as you ask him softly what happened, he bursts into a yowl and tears gush out. Between his gasps for breath you learn that a big boy hit him. Why? Because. Because why? Because I took some bread he was saving. Well, don't take any more bread that big boys are saving!

Another knock. This time it's a little girl, and there's not a tear in her eye, but there's blood all over her leg. She fell on a sharp rock and it cut deeply. Some native kids are very brave when it comes to physical pain. This one was. I picked and dug and cleaned the dirt from the sensitive wound, and she didn't flinch. I told her the iodine would burn, and held her leg firmly so she would not kick, but it was unnecessary. She even grinned when I asked her why she wasn't crying. I pulled all the skin tight with adhesive tape, stuffed in the loose muscles and torn flesh, then bandaged it up. Ten minutes later she was running around the yard playing ball.

The brief medical training I had received before coming over came in handy with the kids. During the six months I spent at St. Vincent's Hospital in Portland, Oregon, under the tutelage of Doctor Blickle, I often thought I was wasting my time. I was learning general medicine, first aid, and how to extract teeth. I even had a course in obstetrics, when all I intended to do was teach catechism to pagans. But now that training often comes in very handy.

When treating the cuts and sores of the natives, even of the children, I've learned to be careful. One of our girls had a stubborn, running sore on her thigh. It was about as big as a quarter, quite deep, and usually full of pus. Every morning she knocked at the door, but no matter how often I cleaned it there was aways a terrible stench to it. My remedies got nowhere, so I took her to our nearest Catholic hospital, the Benedictine Hospital at Nongoma, about a hundred and twenty miles away. There are two other non-Catholic mission hospitals closer but they are not so well equipped as that of the German Benedictines in the neighboring diocese of Eshowe. The doctor gave the girl's sore a quick look and asked how I had been treating it. I told him I had just kept changing bandages. "With your bare hands?" "Why, yes." "Father, I know you priests like to help the natives, but please be careful. Take a good look at this sore so you will recognize it again. You see, syphilis sores are highly contagious. . . ." Gulp!

When I mention a boarding school, don't think that the details of ours are anything like the boarding schools in America. The children's food, for instance, is for the most part a simple diet of corn porridge, three times a day. The children themselves directed by the sisters, do the cooking, outside, in large black iron pots. They take turns feeding the fire, gathering wood from the surrounding bush, stirring the heavy porridge, and dishing it up in tin bowls. Twice a week meat and bread are added to this along with some type of greens. This food is far more plentiful and far more regular than they would get at home; every boarding child puts on weight in the first months, and some actually become fat. This makes good advertisement for our school.

The children's mail, and ours too, comes in and goes out three times a week. As soon as they learn to write they are anxious to send letters home; the parents cannot read but they find someone who can. Then they have this literate neighbor write an answer to the children at school. We pick up the mail at the local trading store, which has a small post office attached

to it. Trading stores dot the bush at about fifteen-mile intervals.
They are usually owned and operated by white people, but
employ many natives for clerks. We buy the children's food
from these stores, drive up with the big truck and load sacks
of ground corn for a two or three weeks' supply. Most of the
food that we missionaries eat we haul from Johannesburg or
Durban. Large quantities of canned food, vegetables from our
little garden, chickens, and the meat from the occasional slaughtering of a cow make up our fare. It must be good because the
majority of us add weight. I myself have become forty pounds
heavier since coming to Africa. We don't cook for ourselves except when we visit outstations where we live alone for three
or four days. At home we have a native man whom we have
trained to cook our food American style.

On week ends and holidays keeping the kids pleasantly busy
is largely a matter of guesswork. I bought a few games and
puzzles only to see them gather dust. The kids have their own
games with stones and twigs and things, games they learned
around the hut and are fond of. They'll monkey with the
checkers and dominoes when I'm looking, but their heart is on
climbing trees and running until they drop. The boys go for
boxing, but not in the same way as our own. There's never a
serious moment with them when the gloves are on. They're convinced it's a foolish way to fight compared with clubs and spears,
so they just play around.

When they first leave the home kraal to live at the mission
some are terribly homesick. One dull Saturday afternoon I discovered a tiny girl hiding herself under a bush quietly crying.
She had been there alone for hours. The diagnosis was simple:
she was homesick, desperately so. Soft, sympathetic talk seemed
to do little; she could think of nothing but her mother, her hut
with the nice fire in the middle, her goats and her dog. I took
her hand and told her how well she was doing in school and how
the teachers and I were pleased with her. Said she had a very
cute face too, when it was clean. A few handy pieces of candy

got her up from the ground wiping her tears. From there I lifted her onto my horse and let her hold the reins while I walked him. She was coming around. Then we went to the storeroom and got a small pinafore. It popped her wet black eyes and blasted away the remnants of homesickness. Subcrisis one hundred and fifty was over.

Clothes are a major item with the kids, mainly because they're so new to them. At home the fire and sun kept them warm. Now, at school, short pants, shirts, dresses — that's just keeping up with the Joneses. Shoes and underclothes are miles ahead. Little guys don a big shirt with long tails, nothing else, and feel well dressed. Girls come with gunny sacks for skirts and sugar-bag blouses. One girl from deep in the bush who came to board with us asked me for a pair of bloomers, on the day after her arrival, just as one would ask to pass the butter. I swallowed, composed myself, then went to the trading store and bought them. When I gave them to her, she turned them over, puzzled, studied them, then looked at me quizzically. "All things to all men," Paul told us priests, but I drew the line at showing her how to put them on. Let her miss a few times by herself!

Early in his job the missionary has to figure out some workable philosophy of clothes with the natives. Their natural dress is scanty indeed. Men and boys wear loincloths, which consist of brief pieces of animal skin — usually monkey — one piece hanging in front and one in back and both supported by a leather thong around the waist. Married women wear a cowhide skirt, heavy, pleated, and treated with some type of blackish preservative. Unmarried girls sport a short skirt — and I mean short, perhaps eight or ten inches above the knees — of beaded cloth. That is all. Pagan women in tribal attire wear nothing above the waist.

When attending church, natives in their natural dress can prove slightly distracting to the priest during the sermon. Still he can't put too much emphasis on clothing; it is secondary. They have their own rigid rules of modesty, and keep them, and they are jarred if we impose ours on them too quickly. Then too, some just don't have the suitable clothes for church; yet they want to worship God at Mass.

The best solution seems to be to let it work itself out. We stress the fact that clothes mean little to God. Clothes or the lack of them should never be a bar to proper worship. When they do come to church and see others dressed more fully, they usually manage to cover themselves in some manner the next time they come.

Every morning after breakfast it's my self-appointed task to have a look at our sick bay. That's a small room near the school where I always find a few kids ill. Next to a little girl who is pretending a stomach-ache and looking for sympathy I'm liable to discover another who is dying with malaria. That merciless disease is plentiful here. Even without a thermometer it's easily spotted: watery red eyes, hot head, shivering body. The kids are great fakers, though, especially the girls. They're crazy about pills, the bitterer the better. Bright colored bottles help too. And fizzling Bromo Seltzer is out of this world. I only drag that out on state occasions, like the time a boy swigged some of the methylated spirits we use for our lamps.

The biggest knock at the door I got was when six of the children overnight came down with chicken pox. It was serious I knew, and could spread to the whole sixty, besides being poor publicity for our school. I acted like a young husband taking care of the house and three kids while the wife is away having the fourth. We hustled them off to the Benedictine hospital immediately. There they were stuck full of needles and quickly responded to modern medicine. None of the others picked it up, and only a few of the more suspicious parents thought we gave the children the sickness for discipline.

If the kids ever get on our nerves I have found the perfect remedy, not for them, but for us: just go away for a while and then come back. A week will do. The welcome we get from them makes up for twice their trouble. Like all natives, the kids too are extremely emotional. Their affection for us may not be deep but it's always bubbling. After we're away for a few days they begin watching for the car. They see it coming up the hill; there's a stunned pause while they recognize it: then pandemonium breaks. They jump and yell, dance and scream, and charge down the road. They can see you like it. Like it? — you're thrilled! So they pour it on, all stops out, at the top of their voices, rhythmically: "Father's home, Father's home!" "Brother is back, Brother is back!"

When you pull up they deluge the car. All you see is black, familiar, excited, smiling faces. They're quiet when you step out wondering what you'll say. You can catch their whispers: "Look, he's thinner; no, he's fatter; he got a new hat; what'd he bring us!" You shoo them all away and pretend you're not affected. But you are — plenty. It's great to be back. Bring on those pesty knocks at the door. You've missed them.

There is the heart of the subtle lure of foreign missions. Everyone wonders why we missionaries love our work, are anxious to get back even while on our vacations home; they can't understand the smiling way we take separation, loneliness, and a certain amount of physical hardship. The answer lies in our paternal relationship to these native people and their heartfelt response to our labor for them. We are priests, leaders, Fathers twenty-four hours a day on the missions. There are no professional hours — no "please call at the rectory from three to five and from seven to nine" — as there are at home. These simple, ignorant, fascinating people look up to, lean on, and love their missionaries, and then almost leap at the Christianity we proffer them. How can the priestly heart resist?

One of our boy boarders is named *Iqiniseli*. I don't know what it means, but to pronounce this Zulu name you must use the famous "click" of the Zulu tongue. We do it, and the natives think we're burping. That *q* is sounded by smacking your tongue on the roof of your mouth. It's a strange name, and Iqiniseli is a strange boy.

My first glimpse of him came while I was sitting on our cool veranda one still morning. He was walking up and down the red dirt road in front of the mission, stick in hand and nothing but a tiny monkey skin loincloth on his seven-year-old body. He would stop, look at me and the house, look at the school children playing close by, then scratch his little head in puzzlement. It was a white man's house, but how come all the native kids were around? He had never heard of school. In fact, this was the first time away from his kraal, which was many miles away in a very backward area.

At lunch time he was still around, so I motioned him over. He saw my wave but didn't move. That's rare, because in this country when white men wave natives hop. Another wave started him moving toward me slowly and cautiously. He was scared stiff. Very softly and gently I asked him his name; fear had taken his voice. His clear, black, deep-set eyes stared at me intelligently. I let him look at me in silence until I saw him relaxing. It's the way with natives. They must study you before they're at ease; it might take two or three minutes of steady gazing. Then I questioned him and learned that he wanted work. No, he did not want to go to school because he never heard of it. Work the men had talked about. You got money and bought things when you had work — that's what he wanted.

Seven years old, he had walked through the bush for miles looking for a job, and owned nothing but a loincloth and a stick! In my amazement I laughed. Then I made a mistake. I told him to come and I'd show him the school and the other little boys. Casually I reached for the top of his tufty head as is my habit with the kids. He ducked violently and bolted off. He stopped when he reached the road, turned and looked at me wild-eyed with fear. The poor little guy thought I was going to hit him. It took half an hour and endless coaxing from the other school kids before he would come back and talk with me. Yes, he'd give this school thing a go. His first lesson was how to use a bar of soap.

For weeks I left him alone so he could get used to the place at his own pace. The twenty other boy boarders broke him into the schedule. His keen black eyes took in everything. Turn around for the "Dominus Vobiscum" at Mass and there was Iqiniseli's face just reaching to the top of the pew, staring up at me. At recreation I'd often see him holding the floor with the other little guys, and they in stitches. His slingshot was always at the ready, and so were his fists and sticks if I wasn't around. When he began grinning naturally and running in the yard as if he belonged I decided it was time to find out more about him. Kids his size don't leave home without a reason.

And neither did he. His story was like one from another world, as so many things are in Africa. Iqiniseli said that he and another small boy had wandered away from home to the main road. A car driven by a native stopped and gave them a ride. Natives like nothing better than a ride in a car, no matter where it's going. Later the car stopped at a small village. During the layover, another native man came up and told the boys to get out of the car and run away or else they would be killed for medicine — the threat of a ritual murder. Iqiniseli, a great guy for running away, took his advice and disappeared into the bush below our Ingwavuma mountain. For two days and nights he hid in the forest, showing himself to no one. The third day he had walked up the road in front of our mission. The other little boy who remained in the car has never been heard of since. . . . As simple as that! I could hardly believe it, but our catechist and cook, both experienced native men, said the kid was probably telling the truth, and was beyond a doubt very lucky. The driver of the car might have been a cohort of some witch doctor, who rather than obtain the victim himself, would protect himself from the police by using another to do it for him. Once he had the live flesh medicine he could remunerate the driver easily. Superstitious natives pay fortunes in cattle and cash to witch doctors who will cure a sickness, curse an enemy, or effect any other of the wonders of their hidden cult.

After that Iqiniseli became kind of a favorite around the mission. Talk about "Nature Boy" — he was it! He was wilder than any of our little fellows. He climbed trees like a monkey, ate leaves, fought fiercely, and scared easily. Father Motzny — then a recent arrival from Chicago in the throes of learning Zulu — and I had new rifles and a flair for hunting, but we would never think of going without our boy Iqiniseli to help. He would enter the quiet bush as cautious as a cat in front of us — he would even turn around and give us a dirty look if we made too much noise. Suddenly he would stop dead, stiffen, reach out a tiny finger to a nearby tree whispering, "There's a monkey." Father Motzny and I, like a couple of big timers, would cock the rifles and try to remain calm and steady. We would look up and see nothing but thick green foliage. The kid kept his finger steady. We looked some more, hard. Nothing. I whispered to him, "Hey, Iqiniseli, do you really see it?" He would nod without taking his eyes off the spot. Suddenly we would make too much commotion and Mister Monkey would take off through the tops of the trees. Iqiniseli would give us a disgusted look and move on through the woods looking for something white men's weak eyes could detect.

Even our native teacher claimed he's never seen a kid like him. In school he was lightning if he decided to think about the abc's, but usually he had his gaze out the window into the trees watching for birds. He was the happiest guy in the chow line. The idea of three meals a day was probably the only white-man idea that he respected. Discipline was another thing entirely, and it was hard to find the proper way to rein him in without crushing his spirit.

The native man helping the sisters to care for our boy boarders came to me one morning with the news that Iqiniseli had run away the previous night. This time he hadn't cleaned his porridge dish, and when the teacher went after him with a little stick, he ran off. It happened about eight o'clock at night, but Iqiniseli is not afraid of the dark. I became worried. I hated to lose a kid with such possibilities. He didn't have a chance to realize the good things he was leaving. So I saddled up my horse, Red, and went after him.

All day I scoured the bush, poking my head in huts, asking the people if they had seen a tiny, bedraggled kid from the mission. When I told them the story, even they were surprised, because native kids usually do not go out alone at night. No luck that day, so the following one I took the jeep and searched in a wider perimeter. It's hard for a native to walk off this mountain without being seen by anyone; the bush has a thousand black eyes and ears. But no one had seen our Iqiniseli. Nothing else I could do now. The girl who helps in the kitchen, Valentine, a sensible, shrewd observer, said he'd be back in a few days. Others guessed he was gone for good.

On the following monday morning, sitting at the breakfast table, hunched over coffee, half alive, I looked out the window and saw our little Iqiniseli walking slowly and hesitatingly up the road toward the mission. There was a genuine thrill in the sight. He came to the back door and looked a wreck. His shirt was in ribbons, mud was caked on his bare legs and arms, layers of dirt were on his face, and he was shivering from the early morning cold. Just before opening the door I had to compose myself. Running away was serious, and I knew the other boarders would be looking on to see what I would do when a runaway returns. Be too easy and the joint would be up for grabs. I made an attempt, but it was impossible for me to look sternly at the scared little guy. The next minute I was rubbing his dirty, cold, tiny hands between mine and we were both grinning. Asked him how he was, his answer came in one Zulu word, *Ngilambile* — "Hungry."

The reason I couldn't find him was that he had taken to the forest. He had not gone home because he didn't want to. I had visited his parents, and they said he never did like to stay around home very long. They were only mildly concerned about him. Day and night for five days he hadn't moved from the thick woods about five miles from our mission. He let no one see him, ate herbs and grasshoppers, and slept under a tree. When he got desperately hungry he chanced coming back to the mission. Since then he's settled slightly. I now have him in the throes of learning "Ad Deum qui laetificat . . ." so he can serve Mass. The only thing on his little mind now besides birds and porridge is when to change the book.

8. More About Kids

TWO years after being given charge of our main station at Ingwavuma, and about four years after my arrival in Africa, I found myself sitting alone in a small temporary shack, hunched over a cup of homemade coffee, looking out the tiny single pane window. This shack was located about twenty-five miles from Ingwavuma at a place known as Kwambuzi. Brother Jack had been working at the building of an outschool here for the past six months. He lived in this shack of fiberboard while he worked on the cement block building going up next to it. It was February 1, 1955, the opening day of the school year in South Africa.

The school, which we were going to call Holy Family School, was not completed, but the roof was on and we did not want to delay the opening another year. What we had for these little rascals was too important. Through the window of my shack I had a good view of the path leading from the surrounding native huts to our two-acre site. (Again, through our good friend, Roy Rutherford, we had obtained this site.) It was nine in the morning and with nervous fingers crossed I kept a steady eye on that path: up it were supposed to come our first school customers.

Soon three scared natives appeared: one woman and two children. I could watch them without being seen. They were nervous and held hands, something which natives seldom do. Their apprehensive eyes darted in every direction. I looked on in won-

derment as they eyed the school building. No doubt about their
fear, which appeared to mount with each step closer to the
school. Yet they were not in enemy tribe's territory. They were
not approaching a white policeman. There were no snakes or
crocodiles around. They were simply going to school. Courageously they proceeded to the school entrance where I watched
the native man teacher we had hired greet them with a big
friendly laugh at their fears.

We had our first Holy Family School children, but I was
still not at ease. In a virgin area like this Kwambuzi, school is
an unknown and therefore a fearful contraption of the white
man. We had fought this. For months the catechist and I had
been covering the area with our sales talks, polishing and adjusting these talks as we went. The introduction was a finger
pointing to the hill where Jack's walls were peeking over the
green tree tops: "That's a school," we told them. "A school is
a place where children go to learn reading and writing. We
ask you to send your children to us." Because I'm white they
nodded to every word I said, but a few years here teaches you
the worth of a native nod. Last year, for instance, at a new
Ndumu school we didn't even get one child the first day; yet
I had received a hundred promises. Now we were waiting for
the Kwambuzi results.

If you had been out stumping with the catechist and me, you
could see why we were skeptical and nervous this first day. Each
kraal had given us a different and wilder reason for refusing
their kids. They're children mentally, these good natives; they
act on instinct, not reason. On the slightest whim or suspicion
of some unthinking father, six or seven children might be held
back from tasting the meager dish of civilization we serve up
at an outschool, to say nothing of missing the banquet of
baptism.

There is a large kraal near our Kwambuzi school which I
cannot pass without a dull ache coming to the pit of my stomach.
It's a rich place: the headman has plenty of cattle, four wives,

a few mistresses, and about a dozen school-age children. He's polite and smily at all times, always gives me a big hello, but consistently refuses suggestions about school. With him all our proved come-ons have failed.

It's pitiful the way his cute kids run up to me, hang around me even when I don't have candy, and cling to every word I say about school. On a visit there I usually park myself under a shady tree on a stump near the headman or at least within earshot of him. Then I call the kids closer, take their tiny hands and talk to them in simple, almost baby-talk Zulu. I tell them how they will learn to count, one, two, three, how they will be able to write talk on paper and be able to look at paper and listen to it talk back. They will play ball with the other kids and eat lots of porridge at lunch time. They're all ears, and so is the old man, though he pretends to be intent on his whittling.

If their attention lags I play the trump card — my watch. Some school children, I say, can even tell time without looking at the sun, on a rainy day. "See this shiny thing on my wrist? Here, listen." I push it up to a dirty little ear. There's a silent pause, and suddenly the kid bursts out laughing. When the man turns around to see what's the joke, I take the chance to get serious about his foolish stubbornness in refusing to let his children attend school. "But, Umfundisi," he says, "if I send you the girls, they will become smarter than the men and no man will want to marry them." And if his girls don't marry, the guy is out a lot of cattle. It is true; this does happen in rare cases, but when you point out the hundreds of times it doesn't, he won't distinguish — not because he doesn't want to, but because he can't.

Girls are hard to get in school for another reason, a thing I could not believe until I had seen it many times myself. As I approached a kraal one day the adults quickly sent a little girl to fetch a clean grass mat for me to sit on; when the girl shyly brought it over, I thanked her gently and asked her to sit next to me. In a lull in the conversation with the older ones I quietly asked her if she would like to go to school. She answered with an even more quiet yes, but said she cannot because she is pregnant. There was no hiding my surprise, I leaned over with popped eyes and took a good long, examining look at the tiny naked thing curled up next to me. Impossible, she could not be more than ten years old, maybe sixty pounds!

I didn't hesitate to tell her and the others, "But you can't be, it's impossible, your breasts have not yet come out." That's a crude Zulu expression for saying she's not old enough for pregnancy; after a few tries I learned to use it without blushing.

One of the older people saw my consternation and explained that the girl was not actually married but she had been promised, betrothed to some young buck who had an eye for the future. This betrothal includes a walloping lot of privileges. The fellow had put a few head of cattle down and was now away in Johannesburg working in the mines to finish off payment. And it was he who sent back orders that she was not to attend school. So our hands were tied.

Boys aren't easy to get either. Parents give boys a lot of freedom, perhaps because they would take it anyhow. They quickly learn to be self-sufficient, to make their own decisions. No use telling the father his duty to send his boys to school, he laughs at you. So the idea is to work on the boys themselves.

If they herd cattle, you've had it. Not a chance of getting them off that job. Cattle are an integral part of native livelihood: their wealth, their security, their daily bread. And God help the herdboy who fails at his job! He gets beaten within an inch of his life.

At Kwambuzi on this opening day we held our breath until about eleven o'clock in the morning; by then we knew we were in. There were nine brave kids inside the room with the native teacher. He had already written *a e i o u* on the blackboard, and they were forming the letters in high-pitched voices. On the unfinished veranda, open-mouthed parents peered through the windows watching the weird goings on. They were bold, these pagan mothers, just to have escorted the children this far. Now they were keeping a protective eye on them and the whiteman's shenanigans. You could even hear them muttering the *a e i o u* business with the kids.

The children were hearing English for the first time: "Good Morning, teacher. How are you? I am fine, how are you?" From there they would move to their counting lesson — baby arithmetic. Then on to Zulu grammar, reading, spelling, writing, and finally craftwork — weaving mats, making baskets. The curriculum would be interspersed with singing, running around outside, and a porridge lunch. By three o'clock the school day would be over.

Next day the number doubled, and the school was on its feet, still wobbly, but moving. Give it some time, years that is, in slow-moving "happy happy" Africa, and it would be turning out Catholics by the fifties.

The dozen or so day schools we have, like Kwambuzi, are really the backbone of our missionary efforts. With these we wedge Catholicism into the thickest bush. And from these outschools we take children to board at the main mission and to continue further in their studies. These boarders in turn become the cream of our future Catholics.

There is nothing like a mission boarding school for training good Catholic native children. It can't be beat for grounding these shiny black pagan kids in Catholicism. When you have them in tow twenty-four hours a day for nine months of the year, they're bound to absorb something. They attend Mass every morning; they stumble along with the liturgical year, remembering certain feasts here and there; they get used to prayer, the Angelus, visits to the Blessed Sacrament. They witness closehand the charitable works of the priests and brothers and sisters around the mission, see us at meditation, office. It's not difficult to distinguish a mission-trained child from the others. In fact, often white people come to us when looking for good, trustworthy servants. Our children are more respectful, more honest, and often more intelligent than the ordinary run of native kids. Some even leave us with a solid foundation of sincere Catholic piety.

But boarders can give awful headaches to the missionary, especially at the beginning of a school year when new kids are trying to fit into the mission routine. It's so different from their kraal life, this round of morning prayers, lessons, organized working hours, recreation, evening prayers. One of my major headaches came after about two months of the school year had passed. Everything seemed to be going smoothly: kids were happy, teachers contented, servants were co-operating. Here and there a gentle reprimand, but nothing serious. It looked as if not one of the kids would have to be weeded, as the older missionaries had always claimed. Suddenly I came across a blooming thistle.

Boarders are not easy to get, so the priest considers well before expelling one. This boy was our biggest, and so were his ideas. When young pagans act up, it's not child's play. Or perhaps, that's precisely what it is usually. Our mission is small and modest, so we were not thinking of beginning a baby nursery just yet. This boy's conduct would have resulted in our having to do just that.

A few days after I had sent him home I received a scorching letter from his father; the father could not write, but he had dictated to a native who could, and then smeared a big "X" at the bottom. He explained who he was, a subchief of no little stature in the tribe; had so many cattle, so many wives, and was highly insulted at the expelling of his son. Furthermore, he demanded that his daughter leave our school immediately: he, his whole family, his whole area wanted nothing more to do with the Roman Catholics.

The letter troubled me deeply. One of our most prosperous outstations is in his area; his anger, spread around, could do harm to our outstation. The daughter too was an exemplary school girl, and a baptized Catholic. For her to go home would mean bad publicity for the school and me, and she would never be able to practice her religion. Instead of letting the girl go home with the messenger from the father, I packed her, the messenger, and our boarding mistress into the pickup and went out to his hut myself. The boarding mistress was a middle-aged Zulu widow whom we had hired to help the sisters care for the girl boarders. She was a trustworthy Catholic who understood native children well, and was zealous to see her people raise their level of civilization through the efforts of the missionaries. A personal visit and the boarding mistress' explanation of the boy's guilt, as well as pointing out the injustice to the girl in taking her away from school — all this might cool the subchief's anger and let us keep the girl.

The boasting in his letter was founded on truth. As we approached I could see that his huts were bigger than usual, his cattle and his wives more numerous. I stopped and fussed with the boiling radiator while the surprise of my visit soaked in. It was a surprise indeed. Everybody ran around the yard, carrying mats and things in and out of the old man's hut. The kids peeked at me from around corners, and the wives whispered about me: they all knew I was the white fool the headman had been cussing about lately. Patience in a white man is new to these people, so I summoned all I had before ducking into the low entrance of the father's hut.

Our greeting was cool but polite. I took my place on a grass floor mat across from the father. He expressed his happiness that I could speak a little Zulu, and I told him what a fine well-built hut he had. During the ensuing small talk two things were taking place: men and women were entering the hut and squatting on the floor around us, some children too, about twenty in all; and the old man and I were eyeing each other thoroughly. He was surprised with my young face, and I was taken with his intelligent look.

When the hut grew silent, he began his litany of grievances against my expelling his virtuous son. I listened attentively and calmly to the long bragging and circumlocution; he talked steadily for perhaps fifteen minutes. After each of his sentences there would be a low, rumbling murmur of agreement from the deep-voiced men seated in the dark recesses of the hut. After a time a rhythm developed between the father and the men: his words, a pause, their approving grunts. He reveled in his eloquence, the old boy did, especially before his own family and a listening white man.

His oratory couched two ideas: his boy should not have been expelled, and he wanted nothing more to do with the Romans. He wound up with a flourish, to which the men's chorus added a resounding "Yebo!" It was my cue. Instead of beginning immediately, I asked the boarding mistress to explain why I had chased his boy. Her Zulu would be better and she was witness to the details of the boy's mishap. She was clear and quick — native women know their inferior and silent place at such meetings. Then in my own hacked-up but sincere Zulu I made a stand for the girl and our reputation.

Inside that hut it was not easy to put across a point. Those suspicious, ignorant, and now unfriendly, black bovine faces were in no mood for *atqui, ergo* reasoning. I was reminded of some of my former examiners in the seminary who had that same attitude sitting across the table from me during an oral philosophy examination. Chickens clucked in and out disturbing us and the dust on the floor. Dogs barked and kids screamed at my white skin. My Zulu was not easy for them to catch, and a few made fun of it right in front of me. Some ignored me completely. The old man, however, listened attentively. When he did not understand me, a question mark would appear on his face. Then I would go at the same idea with another set of words. Two or three tries and the question mark would be erased.

I expressed my sincere regret at expelling the boy. But told him how I was far more deeply upset when he asked that the girl leave our school. This was rank injustice to one of our best children. Why should he punish the girl because the boy did wrong, or because he is mad at the Umfundisi? "When your first wife disobeys, you don't beat the third, do you?"

My three or four arguments marched up and down in front of him, snapping salutes and clicking their heels. Then I came to the point: "I cannot take your boy back to school, but will you please let the girl continue?" He hit the ceiling. "Nege, Nege, NEGE!" That's more than no, it's strong Zulu for never, unheard of, outrageous! He jumped up, sat down, and jumped up again. He raved and ranted around the hut like a beast, striding in front of the men and me, hollering "Nege, Nege!" For a minute I feared rough stuff, and here I wouldn't have a chance. He and the men perhaps thought of it, but they would never dare.

His anger was contagious, not to the others — they sat in mute silence — but to me. I told him that I was not one for him to raise his voice to, let him know he was an unjust old man who would some day be sorry. I told him he took better care of his cattle than his children, and God does not like that. . . . It wouldn't do for him to be reprimanded by me before all his family, so he brusquely asked me to leave. And I immediately obliged. To stay after that would have been far worse. The little girl was crying her eyes out, but the rest were only too happy to see the boss of the house show a white man the door. No one shook hands, and for the first time in Africa I left a native hut without the ceremonial and affectionate good-bys.

Out in the yard, after a little trouble starting the balky pickup, I let the kids pile on for a short ride. They at least were surely for me. The old man noticed it and saw red. He ran over, swung his stick at the kids, chasing them away from the truck and me, and threatened them with death if they had anything to do with the Umfundisi. Round one to ignorance.

Round two went my way the following week when the girl

walked into the mission carrying a note from her father. It said his anger had subsided; he asked my forgiveness for his disrespect and harsh words, thanked me for teaching his son a good lesson — and would I please accept the girl in school? She had refused to eat any food until she went back to the mission. That is a device by which native children demonstrate to thinking parents that they have been treated unjustly. They use it rarely and only with sufficient reason. And it is usually effective with the primitive parents.

9. Death Comes Close

FOR many Americans, Zululand or Swaziland means a region of lurking lions, slimy crocodiles easing into unexplored rivers, towering trees draped with hanging vines, thick lush foliage, large green leaves, chirping monkeys, angry apes, and maybe a Tarzan swinging through in a bikini howling in a mellow voice. It means clustered native villages, bamboo barricades, savage blacks with huge chests, beady eyes, and long knives — and perhaps lost white men in houses on sticks, cut off from civilization, reigning in a jungle paradise.

It's not quite like that, our mission territory in Zululand. But there is some truth in Filmland's version of Africa. Cannibalism has vanished, but there are ritual murders at our very doorstep. Lions are here, but seldom seen. There are heavy bush and croc-filled rivers, but they are known and completely mapped. There are some lost white men (I've met them, and we're lucky they are lost!), but they do no reigning. There are black natives with bulging chests, but they are not allowed to carry lethal weapons. There are thatched huts but inside you might find table and chairs, record player, an innerspring mattress.

After a few days at home, living in the reasonably comfortable house of a main mission such as Ingwavuma or Star of the Sea or Good Shepherd, where we missionaries have running water, home-generated electric light, and high-powered shortwave radios, we have to remind ourselves that we are actually

111

living in dark Africa, the Africa we've heard about. If we should forget, we are sometimes jolted back with a thundering reminder.

That is what happened one day on a picnic from which we were lucky to return alive. The incident occurred at Star of the Sea Mission where I was first assigned after finishing my Zulu classes. It is the most hair-raising experience I ever had in Africa, and I pray there are no more in store for me.

There were only three of us at Star of the Sea Mission at that time, March of 1952 — Father Delehanty, Brother Tim Culhane, and myself. As the school attendance increased we had found ourselves in dire need of sisters to help with the children. Like everywhere in the world, in Africa too, sisters are hard to be found; we can't get enough of them for their inestimable work. So when a group of native Dominican sisters answered our request to visit Star of the Sea with the intention of looking it over for future work there, we rolled out the carpet for them. They stayed a week, four of them, living in the best makeshift quarters we could manage for them in the school.

On one of the days we decided to take them on a picnic. There is a large inland lake about five miles from the mission, called Kozi Bay. A good map will show it located just below the Portuguese East Africa border, about a mile in from the shore of the Indian Ocean. We have an eighteen-foot boat on Kozi Bay which we use for fishing when we can get off for a few days. It's about the only form of relaxation available for us, other than an occasional trip to the cities of Johannesburg or Durban, each of which is three hundred miles from our mission area.

We knew the ride in a boat itself would be a pleasant thrill for the native sisters since none of them had ever been on a lake before. And the shores of the lake are very scenic in the rough lush way of African vegetation. We packed a large lunch for nine persons: the four sisters, Tim and myself, Nzalo — our native catechist — and two of our cook boys. The boat would have quite a load, but it was built wide and roomy. The sisters and all of us were in a gay mood as we piled into the jeep pickup for the short drive to the lake. It was a beautiful day for a picnic. We did not bring any fishing equipment but Tim and I had swimming trunks in case we got the urge to dive in; the sisters wouldn't swim but they did say they would wade in and get their ankles wet. Along with the lunch and ten-horsepower outboard we took two rifles.

Kozi Bay is the home for about two dozen hippos. These huge animals, which like steam rollers, are harmless to those who keep strictly out of their paths, live in the water during the day, floating lazily with their bulgy eyes and large snout showing above the surface. When the sun goes down they come out of the water and roam around on land to feed all night, eating grass and foliage, which they gulp voraciously with their massive jaws. As soon as the sun comes out in the early morning, they slip back into the water. The rifles were brought not for shooting the hippos, which is against the law — they are preserved game. If they happened to come dangerously close to the boat we were prepared to fire over their heads to scare them away.

The sisters were almost like children on the ride to the lake, talking excitedly about going in a boat, and their black eyes popped as we topped the last sand dune and nosed the jeep pickup down to the shore where our boat was docked. The plan was to ride around for a while, have our sandwiches and soft drinks on the far side of the lake, about eight miles away, then leisurely come home before dark. The lake was choppy that day and the little outboard labored with the capacity load, but we stayed close to the shore and bounced along slowly. Tim and I were having a good time joking with the natives about their fears of the water. These people can be excellent company on an outing. They are always ready to laugh, and when they do it comes from deep inside.

After about two hours of putt-putting along, and about seven or eight miles from where we had parked the jeep pickup, we spotted three or four hippos hundreds of yards ahead. The sisters and servants suddenly became frightened, especially when they saw me get one of the rifles ready. Tim told them not to fear, that he would swing the boat around the hippos as he had always done, but they kept their eyes glued to the black snouts showing above the bright sunny surface. When Tim tried to swing the engine to give the hippos a wide girth, the outboard sputtered; he immediately cut it back and coughed into the shore. The natives sensed the alarm in Tim as he did this and their fears grew. We decided to get out and have our lunch right there.

The two cook boys went to work, making a fire and preparing fresh tea. The sisters explored the rugged, uninhabited shore a bit. Tim and I took a swim, but just in the shallow water and with one eye on the hippos. The barefooted sisters picked up their full skirts a few inches and got their ankles wet but we could see they were not enjoying themselves as much as we thought they would; those hippos had scared them deeply. After the sandwiches we packed up to go home. Tim got busy on the balky engine, but it licked him. It just would not perk. It seems in taking it off the boat when we beached, the native boy let it slip into the water and it had got soaked through.

We decided to have the sisters walk directly back to the mission — a distance of seven miles — with the two cook boys. It would be long and unpleasant for them — and surely not a diplomatic way to treat sisters being wooed into staffing our school — but they would arrive home before dark. The sisters seemed only too happy to go by land and get away from those hippos. Tim, Nzalo, and I would try to row the boat back along the shore to the place where we had parked the jeep pickup, which was about seven or eight miles back, and we did not relish the rowing job.

We rowed for an hour or more but everything was against us, the waves, wind, and the clumsiness of the boat. My skinny arms will never be the same after trying to keep up with Tim at those oars. We wasted some more time attempting to get the engine running, but without success. It was beginning to get dark and we were thinking of those hippos coming out of the water at nightfall. Now we saw that we could not row to where we had parked the jeep pickup — it would take hours in the darkness and if a hippo surfaced next to a powerless boat we would be helpless. We were on the edge of a five- or six-mile dense swamp, so we could not walk directly home. We nosed the boat against the shore but could not stay there with it all night for fear of the hippos. Their huge tracks were all over, their cloven hooves had left deep holes all around us, proof of their awful bulk and proof that this was their stamping grounds.

There was no beach. In some places the water was three feet deep at the shore line, and we had the choice of walking in the shallow water either in the direction of where we parked the jeep pickup or of walking back, also in the shallow water to where we had left the sisters, at the edge of this swamp, and where the walking toward home would be comparatively easy. We decided to continue toward the place where the pickup was parked.

Nzalo, our warrior-built catechist, carried the failing flashlight and the two gun covers. Tim carried the .22 rifle; and I had the large-caliber hunting rifle. We secured the boat to the shore and left everything else in it, the picnic equipment, camera, and our clothes. We were going to have to walk in water usually up to our knees but sometimes up to our chests, so we thought it best to put on our swimming trunks, with T shirts and sandals. The walk would take more than three hours. Tim and I were uneasy, but poor Nzalo was scared stiff. Nightfall stirs native imaginations with weird superstitions.

Kozi Lake has a sand bottom, and the walking wasn't bad at first. The shore and swamp were at our left, and the open lake at our right. Most of the time we were wading in the shallow water. There was no path through the swamp. As we walked, the depth of the water changed often and suddenly;

one time it would be at our knees, then we would hit a hole and sink to our chests. Our shins got nicked from the unseen reeds and sunken debris in the water. It was chilly too, especially when the water came up to our chests; and the rifle got heavy carrying it overhead. It soon was so dark that we could see only dense forest blackness on our left, and perhaps for ten yards over the open lake on our right. I began to shiver, and Tim and Nzalo did the same a few minutes later.

But these notable physical discomforts were nil compared to our well-founded inner fears. This was hippo country *cum laude*. The reeds and swamp and desolateness are just what they like. Hippos, as you see them in the zoos back in America may look quite harmless, nice wide jaws for throwing peanuts into on a sunny afternoon with the family. But they can be vicious, especially if they are unduly disturbed or are in calf. Not infrequently, right on the shores of this lake, they have ransacked natives huts at night, and occasionally their huge jaws have crushed natives to death. Two years ago on Kozi Bay a visiting fisherman from Durban had the whole back of his small boat chomped off by an angry hippo, outboard and all. They would not eat human flesh, but they can be killers. In this black water they could surface right next to us and we would not know it until they were on us. The flashlight was wet and just about out. Crocodiles were another fear, although they are not numerous here. However, every time my foot sunk into a hole I imagined that I was stepping on a sleeping croc's nose.

As we navigated this watery pitch-darkness we hardly said a word to one another. When we did speak our voices would crack with tense nervousness that was impossible to conceal. During one period of silence the only sound was that of the water rippling against us as we pushed through it.

After about an hour of this uncertain progress — and with probably another two hours of it ahead of us — as we were passing a clump of reeds growing fifteen yards or so from the shore, the silence was shattered by the low, deep, powerful, un mistakable hoot-hoot of the hippo, coming from these reeds. We could see nothing except that the ripples of water moving from our chests were met by far larger ones coming from the reeds. Instinctively we pushed forward around the reeds and through the shallower water toward the swamp; then took off at full speed along the edge of the swamp. We had not got far from the grunting and bellowing behind us when dead ahead, perhaps twenty yards away, rose another deep rumbling growl. This hippo was not in the water. Nzalo's dim light caught its massive outline on the shore. The three of us spun on our heels, and tore into that black swamp.

It baffles description, this ageless swamp. Thick, heavy, ancient gnarled undergrowth, large pools of stagnant water oozing with mud and slime, huge shaggy trees, sharp ferns, bushes with thorns three inches long, hanging vines, broken branches, fallen trunks, rotting logs. And we hit all this in pitch-darkness. You discovered things in front of you by bumping into them; the bridge of my nose was soon puffed up like a balloon. A hanging vine caught Tim under the chin and knocked him flat on his back. In our frenzied scramble we could not run two successive steps without falling, hard. Many times we ran head-on into large trees. All the time that angry grunting and hooting behind us, as the bulky hippos came crashing after us. Nzalo made the most headway: he was a native and had the light. Tim and I tried to stay together but it was impossible.

Suddenly I found myself alone in that blackness. I fired one shot behind in the direction of the beasts. The heavy charge reverberated through the silent swamp but the crunching crashing sounds kept coming closer. I stumbled ahead some more in the goosh and then turned, and fired blindly behind me again. The rifle had one shell in the chamber and four in the magazine. That's all I had taken because there was no pocket in my bathing trunks. The sound of the gun and the flash from the muzzle just seemed to make the hippos more angry — the crescendo of their hooting and grunting became more violent.

Tim and Nzalo had seemed to have made good headway as I could hear them calling me from deeper in the swamp. They yelled to me to get up a tree, as they had done. I was so nervous, and busy, I could hardly call back to them, but I found a low branch and climbed onto it. They seemed about thirty yards in front of me. I called to them that the hippos were close but I was up a tree and I would stay there. As I said that, the dead branch I was on cracked slowly, broke, and tumbled me into the mud face down.

The noise of my fall brought the hooting closer and louder; the fierce crushing of underbrush seemed right behind me. I got up and fired another shot in the hippos' direction, then stood frozen grabbing the trunk of the tree in complete panic. It was a gigantic tree which a man could never climb, but I senselessly kept jumping at it grabbing it with my bare legs and arms and trying to shinny up it. The sharp, broken bark gashed into my chest and soft flesh on the underside of my arms and legs.

Thank God for Brother Tim. He continued calling to me what to do. I was so afraid I kept hollering back, "I can't," and repeated my insane jumping at that impossible tree. Tim wanted me to run to him. But I could not see ahead and was afraid to stop looking behind from where those low angry grunts were coming. Finally, I heard Tim say, "C'mon, Tommy, you can run through this swamp faster than the hippos." I told them to shine the light and keep yelling, and I took off in their direction. It was up and down again, smashing and cutting my body; the rifle, strapped to my back loosely, clunked my head several times. The flashlight came faintly into view, and soon I stumbled to the foot of Tim's and Nzalo's tree. My strained arm muscles were useless, I couldn't climb an inch. Both Tim and Nzalo reached down, grabbed me under the arms and swung me onto their tree. They laid me on my stomach over the first branch and Tim shouted into my reeling head that I was safe now. I vomited.

We could still hear the hippos but they were not close and had quieted down. Evidently they too had had a tough time. Tim told me that when we split up back there he had run a little way and almost stumbled into another hippo. Luckily he heard the close grumble and there was a good space for running. Nzalo was speechless for the next hour.

There was no doubt about what we should do now. Sit tight. We would not dare move from our perches until morning when the daylight would drive the hippos into the water. The long hard night began. The branches offered no comfortable position. Our burning legs and arms were bruised and scratched; some deep gashes were bleeding profusely. Our swimming trunks and torn T shirts gave no protection against the mosquitoes, malarial and otherwise; this swamp was their home. Bats were swishing around us. The place was probably well supplied too with unseen snakes — mambas, puff adders, pythons.

It must have been about eight o'clock when we got settled in those narrow, pinching, aching crotches; daylight would come at four thirty. There was no chance for sleep, even a nod would throw us off balance. As it was, Tim and Nzalo each hit the ground: Nzalo's branch broke, and down he went twelve feet; Tim, trying to make himself more comfortable, slipped and ended in the mud below with the wind knocked out of him. Both quickly scrambled back up into the tree.

The night was dreadfully slow. We said rosaries out loud, for two reasons: to pray, and to stay awake. And we said them in all earnestness. Along with the monotonous drone of our Hail Mary's the forest itself was alive with sound, strange, weird swamp noises heard nowhere else: eerie raucous calls, sharp squeaking chirps, guttural belches and bubbling, swooshing of birds and bats, and the steady whining of mosquitoes. It was impossible to keep these away from our bloody limbs; they bit at will. One time, through the endless variety of sound, I heard a low rumble and cautiously whispered to Tim, "There he is again, Tim, close!" Tim just as cautiously whispered back with an Irish twinkle in his voice, "Are you sure now, Tommy, that it wasn't Nzalo's stomach growling?" That broke the ice for Nzalo, who hadn't breathed a word since the chase. He burst out laughing, broke his branch, and was still laughing when he hit bottom.

The gray dawn was a most welcome sight as it crept in ever so slowly. It wasn't the time to reminisce, but I did to myself, thought about the vastly different circumstances under which I had seen the dawn break in Chicago circles. . . . We could hear the hippos in the distance slushing back to the water. The gradual light showed us what pitiful wrecks we were, sitting in those trees. My chest was a mass of dried blood under a shredded T shirt; that impossible jumping at the tree had torn all the surface flesh. It wasn't numb any more; it was burning. It was torture to get our stiffened limbs into motion.

Getting back to the shore was comparatively easy in the daylight. We had only penetrated the swamp about fifty yards. Reaching the lake, we continued walking in the water toward the jeep pickup, our wounds burning. In about an hour and a half we reached the dock, climbed into the pickup, and drove home. When we arrived, Father Delehanty, the sisters, and all the mission children were in church praying for us.

Later that day, our wounds cared for, and while Tim and I tried to sleep, Father Delehanty took some boys back to the boat, rowed it home, and brought the outboard up to the mission for Tim to repair when he had recovered. The sisters stayed on a few more days, but later they sent up a letter saying how sorry they were that they were not able to staff our Star of the Sea School. They would have liked to, it was obvious: they were thrilled with the place and the extremely primitive people, and they realized how much we needed them. But they just had too many other commitments.

No one missionary has a monopoly on close calls. Each gets his share, especially at Star of the Sea. . . . African afternoons at the mission are usually quiet and peaceful. Toward six, when the sun has lost its fierceness, and the noisy day pupils have returned home and the boarders are studying, the place eases into unperturbed mission silence. One evening at about five thirty during meditation period in the small priests' chapel at Star of the Sea Mission, Father Fred Reiman, Father Turatti, and Brother Tim sat straight and still. Father Reiman, a Servite from Detroit, had replaced Father Delehanty while the latter went back to America for vacation. Father Turatti was an Italian Servite temporarily assisting us. The small red flame flicked on the altar while the wall clock ticked quietly. Suddenly Father Reiman's body retched violently and he doubled over forward, clutching his abdomen as if in great pain. A few seconds later he had lost consciousness.

Star of the Sea is no place for a sick man. It's sixty-five miles from the nearest bush hospital, and a hundred and sixty-five from the nearest fully equipped hospital, that of the Benedictines at Nongoma. There is no phone for forty miles. A quick decision had to be made: to go for a doctor, the nearest being sixty miles away and about ten hours' round trip; or chance carrying him to the hospital, which meant five or six hours over a torturous sand road. Both courses were dangerous for Father Reiman's life, which seemed to be ebbing with each successive spasm of pain. The trip to the nearest hospital with Father Reiman was decided upon. It was a Methodist Mission hospital with an American doctor and located at Ingwavuma about a mile away from our own mission there, where I happened to be at the time.

Brother Tim improvised an ambulance out of the station wagon by removing the back seat. Mattress, blankets, and pillows were put in. Father Reiman, now conscious, was slowly and carefully laid on top. A native nurse, whom we employ for our mission clinic, would sit back there with him. She was warned to speak up if she noticed his last breaths coming. Tim was the driver, Father Turatti would follow behind driving the small jeep. In the heavy sand the power of the little jeep could help the clumsy station wagon. In heavier sand, Father Turatti's priestly power could help Father Reiman.

At eight o'clock in the evening the two-vehicle caravan pulled away from the mission. The local native stood aghast and sorrowful watching the commotion. They had seen us haul many a sick native off to the hospital, but this was the first white man, and he a priest. They didn't wave or say a word as Tim slowly drove by. I wonder if any said a genuine prayer for Father Fred. If one did, it would be a great milestone, because only three years ago the first Catholic of this area was baptized. There were six hours of first- and second-gear driving ahead, continual bouncing, twisting, turning, grinding; endless shifting, gunning, guessing. The speed is eight and ten miles an hour, often two or three.

The Willys station wagon rode the sand humps nicely. Still with all Tim's caution, the road was merciless toward Father Reiman. Any motion caused him excruciating pain. One time the nurse reached up and tapped Tim on the shoulder motioning him to stop completely. They would have to give him at least ten precious minutes of stillness. Tim flicked his flashlight down at Father Reiman's bearded, drawn face, and watched it somehow manage a weak smile.

Halfway between Star of the Sea Mission and Ingwavuma there is the Pongola River, which is not bridged of course, but there is a small barge poled by a native character named Nkunzibomvu, meaning the red bull. He's an elderly little fella with a sharp eye for women, crocs, and tips — in the same order of importance. If you can find him, and find him sober, you will get across, otherwise you just sit and wait. The river is not wide here, normally about a hundred feet. It has a swift current and is full of crocodiles. The barge is a large, clumsy thing that can be managed by friend Nkunzi only. While you wait for him to come, you become exasperated and are tempted to grab the pole and shove off yourself. Better not though. Our late Father Delehanty, otherwise known as Captain Courageous, one time took the pole in hand, alone, and ended up down the river at the first bend, barge, pole, jeep and all, stuck on the bank — with a big grin on his Irish face.

It was eleven o'clock when they got to the Pongola, and no Nkunzi-bomvu around. After dark he goes on the prowl and is almost impossible to locate. Tim took off on foot to his hut leaving Father Turatti and the nurse with Father Reiman. No one knows how he did it, but Tim managed to find Nkunzi's hut in that black bush, only to learn he had moved from there weeks ago. After a few frantic moments, Tim luckily found a native who led him to Nkunzi's new place. After midnight they were on the barge slowly moving across the dark river, Ingwavuma two hours away.

At two thirty that morning I was awakened by a flashlight shining in my face and Tim's strange voice in my room saying something about Father Reiman. African nights at this mission are cool and good for sleeping, and the whole Ingwavuma house was in deep slumber. I flicked my own flashlight back into Tim's face and saw it was serious. Sleepily sitting on the edge of the bed I got the story from him in brief. A few minutes later we had our generator roaring away, and all lights on. Father Reiman was in a clean bed, and I was gently knocking on Father Ortmann's door to let him in on things. Father Ortmann, from St. Louis, was the superior of all our missions at that time.

Father Reiman had had an ulcer since student days, which has always given him trouble. His face was deathly pale, worn out, strained; he was completely conscious and deeply relieved to be off that road. Still, he and we were worried. Ingwavuma has a doctor, whom we sent for immediately, but the small village hospital is not equipped for major surgery. If his ulcer had burst there would hardly be time to take him on another three-hour drive to the large hospital at Nongoma. In ten minutes the doctor was at Father's side and diagnosed a perforated ulcer; immediate surgery might be necessary, equipped or not. Father was failing fast. We took him the short mile to the small Ingwavuma hospital, and they prepared the operating room.

Brother Jack LeMay and Brother Andy Motsko were sent about a hundred miles away to bring another doctor to help with the operation. If all went well, they would be back in six hours. We tried to phone through but it was Sunday and all the intermediate exchanges were closed. The Ingwavuma doctor would delay the surgery as long as possible; Father Reiman's body might react favorably to the modern drugs. We had to wait it out. It was a beautiful Sunday morning. Our Masses were channeled to him and we had the sisters and mission children saying special prayers.

With his scalpel in hand all morning the Ingwavuma doctor watched for the telltale signs from Father Reiman's body, his pulse, temperature, white count, etc. The earliest Jack and Andy could get the assisting doctor to Ingwavuma would be noon. At eleven the doctor said Father was holding his own and immediate surgery would not be necessary. By two in the afternoon the crisis was over; even the pain had quieted.

Later that afternoon, about five, the Benedictine priest in charge of the hospital at Nongoma, Fr. Ignatius Butz, O.S.B., arrived with an ambulance and two nursing sisters. The doctor was on his way from Durban. He arrived about midnight. It was then decided not to move Father Reiman and not to operate, but to continue him on medicines and watch closely. A week later Father Reiman left the hospital feeling well. He rested at Ingwavuma for another two weeks before returning to Star of the Sea Mission. And he is still there, feeling fine and doing an excellent missionary job.

10. General Checkup

IN FOLLOWING an account of mission experiences as they are described here, the reader might get the impression that the missionary efforts of the Church are something in the outfield: interesting, totally different, terribly long-ranged, lighthearted bits of evangelical byplay. In the minds of some that is liable to happen when serious matters are treated lightly. But, of course, to the Church, missionary endeavors are serious business. And the Holy Father through the Apostolic Delegates in mission fields and they through the local missionary bishops, keep a close tab on our progress.

Along with these ecclesiastical superiors, we of The Order of Servants of Mary have our own Servite superiors. Our Most Reverend Prior General resides in Rome, but every few years he is bound to visit our mission territory. Our present General is Father Monta, an Italian from northern Italy. Early in 1955 he made his official visitation to our missions. He wanted to see and talk to every Servite here and to be taken through the entire territory. You can hardly blame him: much of his Order's means and men are sent here. Hobnobbing through the bush with Roman Generals is another task in the varied, lovely life of the missionary.

At the time of Father General's arrival I had been at the Ingwavuma Mission for over two years and I was getting to know the people well. For weeks I had reminded them of the coming of their distinguished visitor, a great white priest who lives near the pope, who often talks to the pope about the Zulus, and who is even bigger than our own Servite Bishop, Bishop Barneschi! He it is who is coming to visit the priests and brothers as well as themselves. Reckless comparisons to their own tribal hierarchy had them reeling with the importance of the visit.

When our Father General Monta drove into the mission grounds the whole place was prepared. The sisters had their Sunday habits on, the teachers their best clothes, the children were cleaned and standing in hushed order at the driveway. There were dozens of adult bystanders who wanted to look at this great man from across the waters. When he stepped from the car Father Monta was obviously impressed with the silent, awed reverence around him. He looked at them, then at me. I whispered to him the simple Zulu words which mean, "Hello, my dear people." He asked me to say them again more slowly; he repeated them to himself practicing; then in a loud fatherly tone rolled them off to the gaping crowd. He never had received warmer looks in his life.

The next morning Father General sang a high Mass from a portable altar we had erected on the front veranda. The chapel was far too small for our school children and the adult Catholics. Their eyes could not get enough of this dark stocky man "who lives near the pope"; they knelt and stood and sat on the grass of the front lawn, but they didn't miss a movement of the General during the Mass. After the Mass the General came out and distributed individually hundreds of little medals he had brought from Rome. This cinched him with the people. God and grace cannot be touched, but medals can. They can be looked at over and over, hung around the neck, shown to others. And they were free.

Our good native Servite Sisters had the school children prepared for a little show. These can be the funniest or most boring things in Africa. It depends on the mood of the kids. Ours were in high. The show was to last an hour, but the General and his companion, gray-haired Father Taucci, from Florence, Italy, clapped so hard that it went on for two. Cute little seven-year-olders shuffled on stage with that contagious native rhythm, swung their hips, pranced around, putting the General in stitches. The skit that stole the show was put on by a short little guy dressed as a priest, who ceremoniously stepped in front of a small congregation of other tykes, Gospel book in hand, and harangued them in broken Zulu. At first we didn't catch on to all the kids laughing and looking at me. Its significance dawned when the kid stuttered over a difficult Zulu word that I myself always mess up in sermons; the little punk kept hacking it up over and over. Added to this, was his imitation of my most dramatic gestures, which he turned into absolute corn. Then he waddled off the stage head down and arms swinging Chicago style. The General howled along with all the rest. I figured I'd get even with that guy in the next catechism class, so help me! I'd catch him on the Trinity!

We asked the General and Father Taucci twice if they were serious about wanting to visit our Star of the Sea Mission. It's a treacherous ride, murderous on older people. The former Apostolic Delegate, Archbishop Lucas, took a trip down there and barely made it back with his heart still going. Courageously they insisted on going; the General held to his resolve of visiting every house in the world where Servites lived.

Our jeep station wagon was the best vehicle we had for taking them there, and that was in no great shape. Ordinarily it's a four-hour drive, but I stretched it much longer by driving very cautiously over those sandy bumps. Twisting and turning through the thick bush on two sand tracks amazed them. Quietly gentle Father Taucci asked if there were wild animals in the vicinity. It was a giveaway question. He followed it with, "And do you have a gun with you?" I did. Just at that moment we passed a large tree lying at the roadside; it did not ease him to learn that elephants had uprooted it a few days before.

Wild animals were not in my thoughts at all as I talked with them about the territory and the natives. I was listening to a new noise in the rattling jeep station wagon, deep in the engine, and it was steadily growing worse. The dial for the battery showed a continual discharge. A breakdown in this desolate bushveld could be serious; no food, no water, no help. And with such company it would be dreadful. The General's time is precious, Father Taucci is old, and none of us would relish a night in a native kraal. The noise became so distracting that I stopped and opened the hood. Nothing registered — might as well be sanskrit as a four-cylinder engine. Their distinguished faces were glued to me as I got behind the wheel again; all they got was a weak: "I'm sorry, I don't know what's wrong."

We had been on the road three hours, the battery never charging; the sun was plummeting toward the Western horizon, and there were still two hours of driving ahead. Nothing between here and Star of the Sea but native kraals. The headlights made the discharge needle hit bottom; if I left them on the battery would be finished in no time. So I got my flashlight and held it out the window with one hand, and steered with the other. But the expedient proved too difficult because I couldn't keep to the elusive, twisty tracks. Father Taucci, sitting in front and very much concerned by now, if not plain scared, offered to hold the light for me. What an incongruous sight he made with his gray tonsured noble head out the window aiming the flashlight! The noise in the engine became deafening. It was a screeching, scratching, konky noise, not the steady pound of a burnt bearing.

After enduring an hour of this the General's good humor was wearing thin and we were all exhausted. We passed a landmark which told me we were within eight miles of the mission — walking distance. I switched on the headlights, gritted my teeth — to keep them from being jarred loose — and drove as fast as possible without bumping dignified Servites against the roof. Half an hour later we arrived at Star of the Sea and were shaking hands with the priests and brothers there. Father General and Father Taucci had put away their rosaries.

After the greetings I went with Brother Tim to have a look at the jeep station wagon. His practiced eye and ear diagnosed the trouble immediately. Our generator had burned out; luckily it had not given in all at once or we would never have reached Star of the Sea. Since most of our mission vehicles are of the same make, Tim had an extra generator on hand, and in a matter of minutes the change was made.

Next day there was a fine reception for the General, native style. Two cows had been slaughtered, and everybody for ten miles around had been invited. There was even a bush band consisting of four drums and lots of native beer. This would not be the tame school show that he had witnessed in Ingwavuma. It was more adult and more pagan. I watched the General's expressive face as he looked at the men dancers. Their weird gyrations and sharp thumping stomps in the sand were unbelievable to him. Girls beat a steady tempo on the drums and chorused in high falsetto voices. The whirling men answered with wild grunts and fierce looks, their teeth gnashing. The first five minutes of it took the General's breath away. Only after some time did he and Father Taucci settle back as normal spectators. It was a healthy jolt for the General; that first shock of primitive play gave him an idea of what type of people his men are dealing with.

After Mass and breakfast each day of the visitation the General would have a meeting with the Fathers. It would last about an hour and during it we would discuss mission policy, our general religious life, Order rules, and report conversion progress thus far. This is where the General revealed his qualifications for his job: his quick grasp of a situation entirely foreign to him, his clear intelligence cutting through to basic matters, and his genuine enthusiasm for future development. His time and energy and considerable expense in getting here were not going to be wasted.

One afternoon at Star of the Sea Mission we took him down to Kozi Bay, pointed out where Tim and I had been treed by the hippos, and suggested a ride in the boat. He was delighted; we putted around for an hour hoping to show him a hippo, but that day not one would surface and show his huge jaws to the General. On the way back from the lake to the mission, however, we did have a minor thriller.

The limping station wagon began to sputter and cough. Brother Tim was along, and I felt secure in his mechanical ability. I egged the engine on until it finally quit. Someone made a crack about the General jinxing us as Tim calmly got out to look at the engine. He lifted the hood and jumped back with a yell. The engine was on fire! Smoke and flame shot into his face as he hollered for us to get out. And we did, fast, no waiting and bowing to the more dignified first. Blue bellows of flame flashed from the engine, puffed out over the fenders. We scooped up handfuls of sand and threw it in, but the flame was strong, and we could not move in close. We feared a blowup, too. Father General helped throw sand while poor Father Taucci did his part by standing off to the side in the bush praying. Soon the sand got the better of the fire, and a final handful snuffed it out completely.

Tim and I cleaned out the sand we had thrown onto the engine, patched the leak in the broken fuel line which had caused the fire, and drove home with a rather too smug "it's-all-in-a-day's-work" attitude that amazed the two Servite dignitaries riding with us.

When Father General left a few days later to go back to Rome and his cluttered desk in the huge quiet monastery of San Marcello we all seemed to get the same impression: he was pleased with us, there was open admiration for the great work being done, but he was happy that it was we and not he assigned to do it. This strange, African, other-world atmosphere was just too much of a change from his European life. Father Taucci felt this way even more strongly.

11. Deathbed Apostolate

THE bush is thickly populated and medical facilities are very poor. The result is that people die like flies, especially the old ones. Many of these old people close to death are also very close to heaven if we can get to them with the wonderful powers of baptism. Their imaginations are steeped in superstition, their bony bodies are broken with disease, but their tired minds can easily grasp the fundamentals of religion. With willingness and respect they will talk about God, and listen to what baptism does. Being old, and in almost daily danger of death, they have few impediments. Hence we have the Deathbed Apostolate.

Of course there are dangers attached to such an apostolate. If the sick person soon dies, some will claim it was the Roman baptism that killed him. Others might think light of baptism because it was administered so quickly, with little instruction. The dying person himself might secretly confuse it with medicine and agree to it for no other reason than that. Then too, in a certain sense, it's a poor way to plant the Church in a pagan land, considering the future. Nevertheless, it's a banner day for a missionary when he squeezes one by.

Not long after Father General's visitation to Ingwavuma Mission I left that main mission to spend a few days at the Ndumu outstation, the first place built by our Brother Jack. There was an old man at Ndumu whom I was after for our first baptism in the area. He had been living on borrowed time for years, a victim of severe tuberculosis. Still he was not going to be pushed into anything, especially this dipping in the river idea. The more ignorant natives think all baptisms are a dunking in the river. They get the idea from the numerous native sects whose eager ministers seem to delight in dipping female believers.

To slam religion at this pitiful old man would be a mistake, it seemed. He had been around, worked in the towns, served in the Boer War, and did not hesitate to voice his ideas of oppressive whites. But that queasy sound in his throat and the loose skin hanging over his bones warned that he hadn't much time. During an afternoon visit to him, sitting on a mat across from him, I decided to barge in with a few blunt words about his soul. It was a mistake. His wrinkled brows told me to scramble away and be more patient. I did too. Switched quickly to the weather and crops and knocked them both to pieces. Better let the catechist come and talk to this fellow.

Two weeks later Father Jensen, one of our newest missionaries still in the tortures of Zulu lessons, came with me for my regular visit to Ndumu. The first chore on the day before our Mass was to see the old man. Twice the catechist had been out there and had been received well. He said the man was ready for baptism. They're born optimists, these catechists, but missionaries cannot afford to be pessimistic, so I took the holy oils. It would be interesting to witness Father Jensen's reactions to his first native kraal visit.

The man's breath was still coming in spurts, laboriously. Yet he seemed to have more strength, because he was sitting up. Natives are great sympathizers, so there were about eight cronies squatting around the old man grunting back and forth in low tones. Father Jensen's presence had them nonplused. Two white men at a kraal where until a few months ago no white man had been seen! I explained how this new, corpulent priest fitted into the picture; pointed out how the Catholic Church is in earnest about the conversion of the Zulu people, else it would never send more priests. Their eyes popped when I mentioned it was Father Jensen's first visit to a native hut; openmouthed they all stared at poor Jensen — who, quite lost, asked me on the side, "Say, Punchy, anything the matter with me?"

In a few terse exchanges between the old man and me the crisis was over. Yes, he wanted baptism, and he wasn't totally ignorant of what it was. Our catechist had done his spade work well, Baldwin Memela always did. The old man was pleased to learn he would be the first African baptized by the new priest. He got the name Michael. A week later he died.

I have a pet theory about these deathbed baptisms; it's this: they operate on an apparent preordained plan. Everything, I know, is planned and preordained by God, but often His ways are not apparent. Still, when it comes to deathbed baptisms in this bush, it seems God often makes them apparent, even socks missionaries over the head with the fact that He set the thing up for us.

Let me explain before I get too involved. Not seldom, but many times on an unscheduled trip to an outstation I pick up one of these under-the-wire baptisms. One time on my way back to Ingwavuma from a distant kraal where I had celebrated Mass, I passed our Kwambuzi outschool, without any intention of stopping there. It was during the holidays, so the place was empty, no teacher, no catechist, just an elderly pagan caretaker whom we employ when school is out. About two miles after I passed the school, anxious to get up to Ingwavuma, the engine conked out. I fussed with the fuel line, jiggled wires, kicked the tires, had natives who gathered from curiosity from the nearby huts, push — everything; it wouldn't start. So I walked back to the school, made up the bed in the priest's room there, cooked some supper, and turned in, figuring tomorrow I would send a runner to Ingwavuma to ask Brother Marcel to come after me.

At one o'clock in the morning I suddenly woke up and found a kerosene lantern in my face and the caretaker calling: "Father, wake up." I sat up in bed, looked sleepily around and saw three women sitting on the floor near the door. They were catechumens whom I knew well. One spoke up. "Father," she said, "there is an old woman dying near our home over the hill. She will not live out the night. We noticed the light in your window, asked the woman if she would like to be baptized, and have now come to bring you there." An hour and a half later I was kneeling next to the old woman, the caretaker of the school was holding my flashlight on the tiny ritual as I went through the ceremony. The woman died before sunup. No one can tell me that God doesn't keep a close eye on directing His missionaries to these deathbed baptisms.

Another time I was walking home from some fields where I had been hunting guinea fowl. The fields were about five miles from the outstation where I would have Mass the next day. I know the area well, and I just trudged along the path happy with myself, two nice fat guinea fowl in one hand, and my shotgun in the other. Because I was so happy and kind of dreamy I suddenly found myself lost. It was almost dark, and I had no idea which way to go; the path had disappeared. I stumbled around, not really worried because I knew I could not be seriously lost. A small herdboy appeared from nowhere. I asked him to show me the path to our school; they are usually only too happy to do this for a white man.

The boy, instead of walking dutifully in front of me, just pointed and said it was over there and that he would have to be hurrying along. It's rare to find a herdboy in a hurry, and I wanted him to accompany me to the path, so that I would be sure not to miss it. I insisted he come with me. "But, white man" (He did not know me) "my mother is very sick and I must hurry to her with this medicine from the witch doctor across the river. She sent me there this morning." There was a little packet tied to the cord around his waist. He said his kraal was not far, and after he took the medicine home he would come and show me the path. I accompanied him home.

In ten minutes we were at his kraal, and he explained to his relatives how he had met up with me. Leaving the gun and guinea fowl outside, I ducked into the hut to see his sick mother.

She was dying all right — her glassy eyes and noisy throat told me that. The boy explained who I was and I could see that she understood. I said I would say some prayers for her. After the usual three Hail Mary's I sat next to her and talked about baptism, its tremendous rewards, and how easily she could get it; right now in fact, with that little dish of drinking water next to her. She agreed.

I had no ritual with me, so I just blessed the water with the sign of the cross, baptized her, giving her the name of Gertrude, and told her I would be back tomorrow to say some more prayers. I intended to return the next day with the ritual and oils and supply the rest of the baptismal ceremonies; that pouring of the water was the essence, her pass to heaven. When I came back about noon the following day, after my Sunday chores at the oustation, they were digging her grave. She had died that morning. You can call it coincidence if you please — but it happens too often.

Occasionally we are too late for these last minute salvations. And when we are too late often poor Father is in for an awful session of pagan mourning, the like of which he has never dreamed of.

Norah, one of our day pupils and among the first to be baptized at our Star of the Sea Mission, came to me after school and said her aunt was very sick and would like to be baptized. I grabbed her by the shoulders and asked why she hadn't told me this in the morning when she came to school. She had forgotten. I was into the jeep and out to the kraal at top speed, through bush, over fields, directly cross country. Races like these should not be lost. But this one was. Norah's aunt was dead when we arrived; they told us she had died when the sun was directly overhead, about the time Norah was eating her porridge at school. There wasn't a thing we could do, but it wasn't proper to leave immediately.

Outside the hut a few men were sitting, solemn and silent. The women were just the reverse. They gave full rein to their emotions, all stops out. You could see them working into a frenzy, hammy at the beginning, but very real after it took hold. They were never still, up and down, jumping and stomping around the entrance to the hut. They would strip off their shoulder wrap and whirl it into the air with an eerie, piercing shriek; pull at their close-cropped hair, grab their heads, reel around crazily, then slump to the ground in a heap, howling and moaning, long, low, painful moans. Up again suddenly with more weird and forsaken yowls, more grotesque capers. The noise was not unlike that made by caged wild beasts before feeding time.

Inside the hut, where I went immediately, there was a different scene taking place. I crouched through the low entrance and paused while my eyes got used to the dark. The hut was crowded; they had to shift to make room for me. I took my place in the circle around the wall, pulled my knees into my arms and made myself comfortable. The dead woman lay on her side in the center, completely covered with a dirty blanket and at her feet a lot of odds and ends that had been hers: a small kettle, pieces of homemade twine, a snuff box, some beadwork, a broken pocketknife, etc. They all knew me, but I didn't get the big hello I expected. They were surprised, and perhaps a little put out that I had come so late. My first thought was to say a few prayers out loud, but this cool reception told me to sit tight and keep my mouth shut.

With death lying there in the hut, you would think there would be a hush over everyone. Not a bit of it. People kept up side conversations sitting along the circular wall. I say side conversations, because there was always one main conversation going on with the corpse. Each person would shuffle up to the corpse, crouch close by, then wail to it. I regretted that my catechist wasn't with me to catch all they said. They talked to the corpse as if it were alive and would answer. "What did you do this for?" one would ask. "Why did you go? Here you left us, and made us sad. Why didn't you stay until the corn got ripe? It's half

grown now. Look, see how nice it is out there — your own field."
When the first stepped back, another would come up. "But,
Mamma," she would say, "why did you go so suddenly? Here
I had a nice batch of beer put aside for you! I can't drink it
now: it's yours. Come back and drink it!"

One poor creature sidled up to the corpse with a surprised
and extremely stupid look; she was conversationally less gifted
than the others because all she did was repeat, "Hey, Mamma,
what happened here? What happened here? What happened
here?" Over and over, nothing else. Each time the same words
with different emphasis in her voice, and more puzzlement on
her face. The idea of the death slowly seemed to penetrate as
she repeated the "What happened here?" Finally, she jerked
her head with a nod, then quietly came over and took her place
next to me.

There was a short quiet period inside the hut and I recognized
the voice of our Norah outside, she was screaming and crying.
It sounded fake. She came through the low entrance and when
I saw her face I knew her mourning was fake. She, too, took
her turn at the corpse, wailing and asking questions, but not
with the same ring in her voice as the others. She wasn't deeply
affected; this was little more than a distant relative, but she had
to go through the motions. She did her little skit, then sat in
the background with the rest of us, waterless eyes, probably
thinking about her homework, and pleased to see me inside
her hut.

People moved in and out. Everyone who came in spotted me
quickly but didn't pay much outward attention to me. I kept
very quiet and spoke only when spoken to. After a while one
middle-aged fellow came through the entrance whom I didn't
recognize. He had a strained, mean look. You learn to look
closely at faces when you are not sure of the language. He gave
me a shifty glance, then muttered something which he was
sure I could not catch. But I did. He said: "Who invited this
white man here?" He spat the question at everybody with a

slur in his voice; no one answered. Norah gave me a quick look. I pretended I didn't understand the man — even nodded a friendly hello to him when he sat down. But I realized from what he had said that, priest or no priest, I was trespassing. This was native mourning which no white man could understand. They had been polite so far, but if I overstayed my welcome others might get the same idea this man voiced and it would be awkward for me. In a few minutes I moved outside the hut, nodded good-by to some, and went home in the jeep.

The next day at the catechism class in school I blasted the kids on the importance of getting to the priest on time for a dying person.

12. Wise Guys

"C'MON, Umfundisi, say a little prayer for us poor sinning pagans." It was a surprise to hear that request from such a young man, especially here in this hut filled with half-drunk pagan women. I was out visiting native huts only a few miles from our Ingwavuma Mission. The idea was to get more adults into our catechism classes on Sunday after Mass. It was three years since the Ingwavuma school had been opened and kids were flocking to us. With a little persuasion I thought we could gather a few more of these thousands of pagans around us. I looked at the face of this young man who had asked for a prayer. It seemed sincere. In my naïveté I solemnly asked them all to kneel. Something told me I was making a mistake, but I could not see how.

When they got settled on their knees and became quiet I began the Hail Mary in Zulu, answering the second part myself. I started another and saw my mistake, too late. The young man had his head down reverently, but was grinning very irreverently at the women across from him. They, too, were in on the subtle joke. I felt the blood rush to my face and stopped in the middle of the Hail Mary. They all burst out laughing at me. "But continue, our dear Umfundisi," he urged unctiously. "We are simple natives and need your good prayers." They laughed some more. I wanted to punch that flat nose flatter! They saw the anger in my face, and were delighted with my confusion as I picked up my hat and stick and crawled out the entrance.

That was my painful introduction to an abominable class of natives whom I now know as the wise guys of the bush.

Izighebengu is the Zulu word for them, the equivalent of "sharp-ies," "hot shots." They are usually young men in their early twenties, unmarried, who have been to Durban or Johannesburg, have got a little money and flashy clothes, and now have come back home to show off. They get their spectators too: the younger boys look up to them with hero worship, imitate their cocky swagger and the tilt of their broad-brimmed hats. Marriageable girls coyly admire them — and often a few months later are sorry for their glad-eye glances. Even parents don't ignore them, because their girls must marry someone — and it might as well be a fella with white-man's trousers and shoes in his hand. (In his hand because they murder his splayed feet!)

To the missionary, these wise guys are the bane of his work. City life and pocket money are far too heady for these simple kids. The result is they quickly acquire a veneer of urbanity and many bad habits. On their vacations back home to the bush they teach these to their country cousins. Everything the missionary has been driving home with gentle patience is shattered by their knowing ironic smile and sarcastic remarks about the white people and their foolish religion.

During the sermon at Ingwavuma one Sunday morning I noticed about four of these characters in the back of the room. I, after being bothered so much by them, have a nose for them, can spot them in any crowd. These boys were looking up at me now, boldly attentive, seeming to hang on my every word. I tried to figure out why they had come; I knew it wasn't for Mass. When Mass was over and after I had forced myself to greet them and pass a few kind words with them as I mingled among the parishioners, I still didn't have a clue as to why they were there.

Later, while having my eggs and coffee, the head teacher of our school bolted into the kitchen and excitedly told me these boys had left church and taken up positions in the bush about a block away. They were waiting for a certain one of our older girls to come through that bush on her way home. I saw red.

But there was not a thing I could do. They had a right to the bush since it was off our property, and I had no right to the girl. Ten minutes later, standing on the porch, the catechist and I listened to the screaming and laughing and hollering coming from that bush. We agreed that there was nothing we could do, and that it would be better not to get mixed up in it at all. Perhaps they would not do any real harm to the girl because if they did, her parents could turn them into the police. But they could do everything this side of real harm. And probably did. The screaming lasted for about half an hour. Next day the girl was back at school calmly studying her abc's and the Ten Commandments.

Like certain teen-age groups in America and elsewhere, these bush hot shots move in groups, and while together they are at their worst. Underneath, and when alone, many of them may be good simple natives. I had proof of this when out visiting kraals around Ingwavuma. I came across an old man lying on the ground near his hut. Beside him were two elderly women sitting in their dirty skin skirts, one weaving grass into a mat, the other crushing kernels of corn between two worn stones. The old man's face was a mass of blood, some dried and hard, some fresh and running. Not far away was a group of these young zoot-suiters lounging around smirking at my concern over the hurt old man. I avoided looking at them, for fear of getting angry. Instead I tried to get the story about the old man out of the two women next to him.

It seems, they said, he had a freak accident. He had gone to a small field near his kraal to do some hoeing. His pitiful looking garden is full of large stones. Climbing over one of these he dropped the big rusty hoe in front of him, blade up, then fell face first onto it. It cut his nose and upper lip in half, and made a deep gash in his forehead. That was two days ago, and he had been lying there ever since.

I asked if the women were his wives. No, they weren't, but his son was that young man sitting over there with the others.

One of them, for my benefit, had taken out a packet of cigarettes and was clumsily lighting one. Composing myself I went over to the boys and asked which was the man's son. They laughed at my Zulu. I asked it again, looked at them hard, unable to conceal my distaste for them; there was a threat in my voice as my blood rose. One adjusted his hat, grinned disgustingly, and mumbled that he was the old man's son; his tone of voice as much as said, "And what business is it of yours, White Man?"

They all chuckled again when I suggested that his father be taken to the hospital — he was very old and looked seriously injured. They even made a few cracks about white doctors and their healing power being far less than that of native witch doctors. "Well, aren't you going to help your father at all? He's in great pain," I said. "Listen, my dear Umfundisi," the son said in an annoyed tone. "He's my father, black skin like me, and I'll take care of him. We are expecting a witch doctor in a few days. . . . Don't you have to get back to the mission for prayers or something, Umfundisi?" My blood boiling violently, I left.

That evening I thought constantly of the old fellow lying out there in pain, with his wounds becoming more septic by the hour. But that punk of a son had tied my hands; I couldn't touch the father without his permission. He could get me into trouble with the police, and would only be too happy to do so.

Next morning, still uneasy about it, I hit on a plan. I filled my pockets with soap, iodine, bandages, a safety razor and a clean washrag; also a dozen aspirin tablets and a package of cigarettes. Perhaps the son would at least allow me to clean up the old man. When I got to the kraal, the father was still lying flat on his back — he hadn't moved all night. The two women and the son were there also, but the other young guys were not around. The son was bending over the old man. As I approached I could see what he was doing. He had a small can of dirty motor oil in one hand, and a chicken feather in the other. He was simply swabbing the old man with used crank-case oil from the neck up.

The son's face this morning didn't have the same smirk as yesterday, though he did not greet me with any warmth. I asked him how the old man was and offered the boy a cigarette — anything to stop his garage mechanic's maneuvers over the old man. That little white cigarette seemed to work wonders. It made his veneer of sophistication peel right down to the goodness underneath. He looked at me naturally and with some respect in his eyes. Thank God none of his pals were around! Yes, he would be very pleased to let me clean up his father today, and was even more anxious to have me pour in white-man's medicine. He would help me too; so would the women.

He got a good fire going under one of those familiar three-legged black iron buckets, the kind cartoonists use to roast missionaries in. The water was not clean but it was hot. Washing the wounded man's face was far from easy. The dried blood and mucous were thick and crusted. All were mixed with the stiff hair on his upper lip, and everything was coated with dirty oil. The soap and hot water gradually worked in and showed how deeply the blade had penetrated. His nose would never come together again because one nostril was simply not there. The cut on his head was ragged and deep but was not hard to clean.

The son was a real help, and could hardly be recognized as the brat of yesterday. He got the place hopping. Water is scarce in these hills, but he managed to get plenty. He kept the old man calm too, holding his head still while I shaved around the wounds and picked out the debris. Fleas and other creeping things changed their allegiance from the old man to the young priest. When one bug crawled into my shirt pocket, the son saw it and cracked that perhaps it wanted to go to church. The nursing job took almost two hours. The poor old man took all our clumsiness without a murmur. Only once or twice did he open his eyes, and they were full of gratitude. And so was the wise guy son when I said good-by to him.

The missionary is used to dealing with the ordinary country native, who is simple, humble, friendly. The ordinary native has the utmost respect for a missionary even when not interested in religion, and such good people can become a genuine joy in his life. The "wise guy" capitalizes on this situation. He cunningly pretends that he, too, loves the missionary, admires his work; then suddenly lets Father drop through the false bottom.

When I come up to a group of huts and people whom I haven't visited for some time, it is my custom to greet them by shaking hands all around. The elderly people like it and the children are pleased and astonished to touch a white-skinned hand. Inevitably the kids whisper to each other, "How soft the Umfundisi's hand is; and it has fur on the back!" In entering a particular hut one day I came into the presence of about seven or eight people, most of whom I knew and liked, though they never come to our church. Our greeting was pleasant. There was present a young man who didn't look like a proper wise guy, but was. I shook his hand last. When I touched it, he took a firm grip on mine and squeezed hard. He was a husky lad who had been working in the gold mines and had more strength in one hand than I had in both legs. I jerked my hand away before it got painful.

Instead of sitting down on the mat they had placed for me, I stood back, made an awkward silence, then slowly eyed this fellow up and down. They all knew why. He didn't wither before my gaze, but he wasn't comfortable either. I had often called down his kind before — it's not a difficult or brave thing for a white man to do in this country — and I took my time, thought over well the Zulu I would use on him. The words were not choice but they carried the point. I told him what a dreadful blight he was on his good family, and what a prime, pretentious ass he was to ape Europeans, and give up his own wholesome native habits for their bad ones. The head of the hut gave the nod to everything I said and ordered the boy away. He obeyed too. We sat down and had a nice visit.

These would-be delinquents are an endless source of trouble in a mission where there are girl boarders. Maybe it's not always the boys' fault; our sweet-singing, fervent-praying lasses no doubt keep their eyes peeled and use them well. Not long ago we American Servites had a get-together for our schools, a three-day tournament here at Ingwavuma. In the evening the children were to sleep in the classrooms, boys in one, girls in another. All day there were plenty of these local sharpies around watching the games and girls. As it got dark everyone was supposed to leave the grounds except our own school children. We priests and brothers left the kids to themselves while we feasted and gossiped about everyone back in America.

I expected trouble from a certain group of these floaters, whose eyes had been bulging at the fair sex all day long. Before the kids' bedtime, about nine o'clock, I strolled around the school with my flashlight and spotted the group hiding themselves in the bushes near the school. With all the kids from the other school visiting us, our facilities were crowded, so those bushes would be used occasionally. The wise guys knew this and were waiting. Pretending not to see them, I went back to the house and got two good helpers — a big stick and my revolver.

The idea was not to hurt them or even catch them but just give them a healthy scare so they would go away and stay away. I circled the bush with my flashlight turned off and came on them from behind. They didn't see me. When I got close I flashed the light and ran in at them thrashing with the stick. In all Africa there probaby were never five more scared natives! They screeched and scrambled and took off at full speed. To assure them doubly that they were not welcome at this hour I fired two shots in the air. We had no more trouble with them that evening.

13. Horse and Rider

THERE are two skills of great importance to the Zulu missionary, which most west side clods from Chicago know little about. Here they are in their order of magnitude of grief to a citified missionary: riding a horse and driving a big truck over Zululand roads.

Of the five or six horses I've had at different missions "Red" is the most celebrated in my mind. He is now dead — but this is not his eulogy. He was the first horse I ever had, the first I ever rode, and the first I saw die. Horse sickness swept Northern Natal a few years ago and I was sorry to see it sweep Red. Still, for me, there was little sentiment in his passing; I suppose I haven't seen enough Television Westerns to appreciate a horse. And besides, that nag threw me too often for sentiment. He was handsome, a good runner, and a good old plug in general. But he had absolutely no respect for the cloth.

It was at Good Shepherd Mission at Hlabisa, about five years ago, where Red and I first crossed swords. Here at Ingwavuma Mission at the present time I have a second horse named Red, but he is not to be confused with the original. This Ingwavuma Red is a gentleman through and through.

The steep and ranging hills around Good Shepherd Mission were wearing me down. The local natives had a few horses and mules to scale them, and for months I watched them with envy ride bareback while I trudged along on foot. Often they would pass me on a difficult rocky path leading up the side of a hill and would suggest, "Umfundisi, why don't you get yourself a horse?"

I broke down and did. In a local farmers' magazine I noticed an ad for riding horses, sold from a stable about two hundred miles away, at a town called Bloemfontein. I would have liked to see the horse before buying, but I knew that my knowledge of horses was limited to western movies. So I ordered the horse to be sent by rail, and had one of our day laborers, a native man who said he used to care for horses, go to the station, thirty miles away, and ride the horse to the mission.

Red and I began our feud the first day he arrived. He looked at me with searching eyes and saw me for the phony horseman I was. I looked at him and knew only that he was a horse. Brother Tim, who knew horses and could show me plenty about riding, was a hundred and twenty miles away on his own mission at Star of the Sea. At that time Brother John Bardini was the only one with me at Good Shepherd Mission, and he was more ignorant — and more scared — of horses than I. The new horse and I were left alone to figure things out. I had a shiny new saddle, new bridle, everything, but only the vaguest notion of how to put them on. It was hit and miss until the gear was strapped on correctly. Red grew more angry by the minute. Watching everything closely was a group of our school children, terribly interested in seeing their priest get on a horse. Their presence didn't help my nervousness. I put one foot in the stirrup, swung the other up, and Red nonchalantly stepped away. The spill caused a huge guffaw from the native school kids. I had a boy bring me an apple box to stand on. It gave me the needed height, but just as I was swinging up, Red with one stroke calmly kicked the box to pieces under me.

It was an inglorious beginning, but worth the effort. After a week Red and I became compatible and I found myself covering distances I could never manage on foot. Those first weeks I wouldn't dare let him have his head, and we wandered through the bush slowly. Red's worth to me showed immediately, we visited huts and saw people that I never knew existed. These new faces got a laugh out of my uneasiness in the saddle, and at times, my abject fear up there. Natives are used to riding — horses, mules, donkeys, anything — always bareback. Some have these animals as their own property, others have cared for them on white people's farms. The natives have an excellent technique in dealing with animals. Most white South Africans are excellent riders. No one could understand my holding the reins so nervously, hardly moving, pleading with the horse not to go fast, and please move this way or that way. Once I became cocky and learned what a dreadful mistake it was with Red. I gave him a sharp tap with the whip, and he bolted into high gear. Ten steps later he turned quickly and I continued on forward, without him. While I picked myself up, he stood quietly munching on nearby grass.

The more I rode, the more I learned about Red and his usefulness. If a catechist is the right arm of a missionary, in this mountain country a horse is the missionary's legs. Hills that used to murder me on foot Red would take in a few puffs. He could cut cross-country, through swamps, stickers, rocks, while I just sat on top and bounced along. He didn't mind how heavy my lunch in the saddlebag was, so I ate better than when I had to carry it while walking. I could carry more medicine, too, for the common aches and pains I would run across with the natives. And on my visits with them Red was always a good conversation piece.

In a strange way too, he saved much of my time. On foot, when I approached a new hut with a come-to-church sales talk primed, native etiquette decreed that I linger a while even though I could see I was unwanted, or at least that I would never get any churchgoers. On the horse, however, I could size up the place before slipping off the saddle. If I saw that the atmosphere was not ripe, I would remain on the horse and move on. No one would be offended. It was smoother, diplomatic enough to satisfy all, and took so much less time.

Red quickly caught on that I was delighted with his work, and that I needed him for mine; so he played hard to get. By that I mean he got ornery. In all his six years of life I guessed he had never had it so soft: a lightweight rider whom he could pitch at will, who was afraid to make him run, afraid to use the whip, and who gave him plenty of food. What other horse owner would let him get away with all this? He began his revolution by refusing to cross small streams — which are plentiful in places. After trying what little I knew to persuade him, I ended up by leaving him tied, wading across on foot, and walking to my destination. Coming back to the stream, I would wade across again and climb up on Red. He also began to refuse to cross country, declaring a paths-only policy. It even got to a point where it was hard to get the saddle on him in the morning. Finally there was nothing to do but go and have a long talk with Tim. Horse-wise Brother Tim told me all, and I listened well. The essence of his advice was this: "Tommy, take no guff from any horse!"

The following Monday morning I went at Red with a chip on my shoulder. He had got into the bad habit of bloating his stomach while I tied the girth, the result being a loose saddle — very dangerous. Tim's remedy was simple: a blow in his belly with your knee to knock the wind out of him before adjusting the girth. What an awful way to start things on a Monday morning I thought — a kick in the belly — but it worked. At the first stream there was a showdown again. Tim's instructions were to use the whip, hard. When Red stopped at the water, I gripped him tight with my bow legs (I knew they'd come in handy sometime!) held the reins close and firm, and belted him with the whip. He jolted me terribly, but never touched the water. His big head came around slowly with ears cocked, and he looked at me as if to say, "What in hell's aching you, Padre?" Another belt — with all I had. He waded across.

One time we had a narrow escape which Red knew more about than I. We were about ten miles from home when we finally arrived at the river I wanted to see. I was looking for decent sand deposits for making cement blocks. It was a desolate area, no huts or natives around for miles. I got off and led the horse to the water for a drink. While he slurped I noticed some huge deep footprints in the soft sand. My own shoes sank about an inch into the sand, Red's about two. The large hoofmark was about six inches deep. It was a four-legged something which had come out of the water and walked along the bank. I knew there were no elephants in this area — they were more than a hundred miles away. I thought of hippos, but they too had never been seen at this spot. There was a .38 revolver in the saddlebag which I slipped into my pocket, then walking in front of Red I led him along, following the strange tracks.

It was wide open all around so I wasn't afraid, just curious. Red stopped and lifted his palpitating nose. We were a short distance from some bushes into which the tracks ran. I gave the reins a little pull urging Red on, but he jerked back his head and refused to budge. He stood with his head high and nostrils dilated, obviously frightened. I left him and walked a little closer to the bushes into which the tracks led. Not a sound. The noonday sun was beating down hard and hot. No breeze stirred. I approached to within about ten yards of the thick bush then listened closely. Dead silence. A step closer and I heard a gigantic sigh. It was hardly audible, but enough to tell me something was in there and it was big. I moved away silently, got on Red quietly, and took off at a gallop.

Back home that afternoon I told the incident to our cookboy, an elderly native who knows the country well. His eyes dilated like a Harlem Evangelist; he told me the Lord Jesus was with me, and how! This time of the year that place is a haven for rhinos. That's why there are no natives around. The rhinos walk down the river from upcountry; on hot days they snooze in shady bushes along the bank, and no doubt dislike being disturbed!

Not long after this I noticed Red slipping. Pull the reins to the right and he went to the right; to the left, and he went left. He must be sick, I thought, obeying like this. Around other horses, including mares, Red couldn't care less. Before now it had taken all I had to hold him. Finally he stopped eating. We never were friendly, but he would always take a handful of sugar from me.

All the natives and the local white storekeeper sympathized with me about Red's sickness. They knew it was fatal. He had contracted a horse disease common in South Africa, which is simply called horse sickness. The upper part of the horse's head swells, as did Red's, and he becomes very listless. I sent away for the serum, which took about three days to arrive, and injected it myself, a double dose. But the natives continued to say he was on his way out.

One hot afternoon the school kids came running up to tell me my horse was lying out in the field. When I got there his mouth and nose were frothing and he was hardly breathing. I waited a few minutes while he puffed his last and was motionless. Then I stepped close for a good look, the only time I got so near the beast without any fear. Suddenly his front leg muscles shivered with reflexes, the leg stiffened quickly and his hoof crashed into my shin for a painful bruise. After that Red never stirred. That last kick proved he died as he lived, a confirmed anticlerical.

Driving a big truck is not as necessary to a missionary priest as riding a horse, but it does come in handy. A main mission is usually equipped with a five-ton truck. You have to have one for building, and missions are always building. Sand water, cement blocks, timber, roofing — all these must be hauled to the building site. There are some cartage contractors in the Union of South Africa, but they would laugh if you asked them to come to this bush. So we must depend on our own trucks, and our own men to drive them. The brunt of this driving of course falls to the lot of the lay brothers, but the priest is not exempt.

At the Ingwavuma Mission we have a large truck, but there is no need for me to drive it much because there are three lay brothers here; the only time I take it out is when I have a picnic with the school kids at the Ingwavuma River, about twelve miles away. When, however, I was stationed at Star of the Sea Mission with the late Father Delehanty and Brother Tim, truck driving for the priest was a must. It was far more difficult in that sand country, and Tim could not be expected to carry the whole load. The trip from Star of the Sea Mission to our nearest railroad terminal of Mkuzi — the Mkuzi Run, we called it — was a grueling all-day session behind the big wheel, in a hot cab, over eighty-five torturous miles of sand — one hundred seventy miles round trip.

For such a task everything is prepared the night before: truck gassed, oiled, watered; sandwiches, tea, and drinking water put into the cab. In the back are loaded planks, shovels, bush knives, and a tarpaulin, also an extra gas tank and can of water. This is all standard equipment for the Mkuzi Run; none of us would think of going without it.

An early start is essential; so when I am to make the run, I rise about two-thirty, celebrate Mass at three with my two native laborers who are to help me load. We don't start the generator for light because it would wake up the others. Seems strange to be saying Mass without a lot of noisy, sniffling, coughing school kids behind; the quiet is almost eerie in that candlelight. The hot coffee tastes good at that hour. I drink it standing in the kitchen. Out to the truck, warm up the engine, switch on the lights, shift the heavy gears into first and move off the mission grounds.

Eighty-five miles doesn't sound like much — Chicago to Milwaukee, no more than two hours. But here there is no Highway 41. The so-called road is nothing but twin tracks of soft sand with tall grass between and bush on both sides. Few people besides ourselves and an occasional police jeep use it. The sand looks smooth, but it's treacherous and unbelievably bumpy.

You can never go more than ten miles an hour, and often you go hours in first gear at five.

Through the steering wheel I can feel that the sand is loose and heavy. I hunch up and strain my eyes into the headlight beams watching for the bad patches. It would not be hard to get stuck with the truck empty like this — no traction. All I really know about driving this big thing is to keep it going, gun through everything, because once stopped in this sand you sink in right to the hubs. The seminary never offered a class in five-ton trucking; and St. Thomas has nothing in his books about double-clutching in low-low. (Or does he now, Thomists?)

Three miles from the house I see a lot of loose sand on the approach to a small hill, a bad spot that caught me before. I quickly shift down a gear, push the accelerator till the motor's screaming, and go tearing at it. It is only about a twenty yard patch, and I have a lot of speed and power. The truck grinds, vibrates, lurches, and then spins to a stop, the whole differential buried in sand.

The two lorry boys (as we call them here, taking after the British) know their job and need little direction. They take off the planks, shovels, and bush knives, start clearing the loose sand from the rear end, while I hold the flashlight for them. When it's open enough, they hold the flashlight and I put a plank down, adjust the heavy hydraulic jack under the axle, and slowly lift it up. The gaping holes where the back wheels spun we fill with underbrush and large palm branches; then we do the same with the remainder of the bad patch ahead. The boys stay down to push when I start. Sometimes a few boys pushing makes the difference. I gun it again, lean over the wheel, and out we come, bounding onto the harder sand ahead. The boys throw shovels and planks back on, hop up themselves, and we continue to Mkuzi. About an hour has been lost.

It's not all heavy bush country between Star of the Sea and Mkuzi. Much of it is broad gently rolling plain with a little parched vegetation. The powerful headlights sometimes catch the shining eyes of a small deer, a rabbit, the sliding form of a snake. They also show you sand-bear holes, which are dangerous for the truck. They are holes in the road, small on top, maybe six inches, but large and deep underneath; they can swallow a whole wheel in one gulp. Hit them fast and you break the axle. The sand bears — a large species of anteater — dig them quick and often, so that yesterday the road might have been fine, but today there are three or four where you don't expect them.

We usually take three lorry boys, who are actually grown men, husky for the work of loading. Two ride in back, and the other sits up with the driver. The long hours on the road are often pleasantly broken by a genuinely interesting conversation with these men. Even though the Zulu is somewhat laborsome for me, the subjects talked about become so absorbing that you find yourself not even thinking about the words.

The individual Zulu, talking freely, can become the best company. One fella, as he would gripe about keeping peace among his three wives, would double into a belly laugh. "Ya know, Umfundisi," he would say "maybe you Catholics got something there in permitting only one wife to a man. Man, sometimes I wish I never had any! I buy a new hoe for one, and the other two want new ones too. They would never use them if I got 'em!" Another would complain that his wife never puts enough sugar cane in the home brew, so that when he comes home after one of these Mkuzi trips, he drinks all she has and doesn't even get loaded!

We talk seriously too. They think I'm going to give them a conversion sermon up there in the cab, and when they find I talk about everything else but religion, they themselves often bring it up. "Why, Umfundisi, how come God made white and black people? When we all get to heaven, are the black people going to work in the kitchen all the time? You say you came to our country in one of those flying motor cars; could you see heaven from up there in the clouds?" I make my answers simple and direct. But I prefer to probe deeper into their own unfathomable tribal life.

Driving at this early hour of the morning is not bad because it's cool. You feel good. The morning star is hanging over there on our left, out the window to the east over the Indian Ocean. "Jam lucis orto sidere" would come to mind if this endless shifting and steering weren't so demanding. Slowly the darkness gives way to that early gray. I switch to the dim lights and wonder if it will rain today. Rain is great — it makes the sand hard and fast for driving. A little later the sun sneaks up, and I stop for a sandwich, some water, and a short walk. The boys relax too, some roll a rough cigarette from a piece of brown wrapping paper and home-grown tobacco, others reach their hand into a billy can for some cold porridge their wives prepared.

Fifty miles and five hours later we arrive at the foothills of the Ubombo Mountain. Ten miles the other side of this mountain lies Mkuzi. On top of it we have a little outschool with priest's quarters. The road goes right next to it. It is a great place to stay if you break down. Ubombo's not a high mountain, about two thousand feet. The motor whines and whirs violently as I let the gears hold the truck back going down the other side. At about nine o'clock in the morning Mkuzi comes into sight, a frontier town, not unlike those of our early west.

The town doesn't have Gary Cooper stalking up the main street toward the varmint behind the swinging doors, but it does have an unpaved, dusty main street. The old trading store occupies the center. There's a garage, and a broken down native recruiting station down the way — recruiting for boys to work in the gold and diamond mines. Motley groups of natives are lounging around, others are crossing the middle of the street with huge packs on their heads, kids playing, mules lumbering under heavy double packs, cows, chickens, dogs milling about. There are a few white men in western dress with large brimmed hats, carrying supplies to their dusty pickup trucks. These are from the surrounding farms. Then across the road from the general store is the only other hub of activity in the town, the rail station. A narrow-gauge Toonerville Trolley rumbles through here once a day, stirring the place into a semblance of activity. Some natives walk for miles just to get a look at this iron horse. On big feast days we sometimes bring our school children here to give them a glimpse of it. They go home talking about it for months, even carve wooden images of it.

Getting loaded at the rail station shed is not a simple matter. It's complicated and exasperating, and cannot be done in a hurry. Nothing can in this country. Just saying hello to the locals consumes time and tea. Tea is a fetish here — tea in early morning, midmorning, noon, low tea, high tea. Sometimes I drink so much tea for politeness that when I walk away I slosh! The rail shed is unbelievably confused. And all the while you are trying to get things organized you know you will be that much later getting home to the cold shower and cool veranda back at the mission. A few quick half crowns in the proper black hands other than those of our own boys and the truck is usually loaded in a jiffy with whatever it is you came for.

After loading I drive to the broken down garage for refueling and checking. This is the only garage for a hundred miles around, so the policy is always to be friendly with the mechanic. Especially do I, the world's worst mechanic, treat him with kid gloves. Sure, I can roll off the terms — "Had trouble with my throw bearing the other day — felt like throwing it out; condenser's kicking up too; cam shaft is not camming" — out of the side of my mouth like a veteran. But it's all baloney and I know it. The lorry boys, while I visit and buy odd supplies, usually spend a few shillings buying handfuls of sugar or rice or ground corn. They meet many of their cronies there too and have a few drinks of native beer together; but not too much — they have to keep a clear eye on the load going home. All three ride in back then.

About noon I pull away from Mkuzi. The trip home is pleasanter, mainly because half the job is finished. The driving itself, however, is more work. Clutch and gear-shift lever never rest and neither do you with those five tons of dead weight at your back. Climbing up the mountain is slow. The truck is powerful and will make it if nothing goes wrong; so you just put it in low-low, and it growls its way up. Going down the other side the noise is deafening as the five tons lean on the gears. The engine whirs into a roar, and you tense up over the wheel guiding it down the narrow winding road. There's a thousand foot drop on one side.

It's good to get off that ticklish mountain and onto the flats. I relax, sit back in my wet T shirt, spread myself out in the driver's seat. The sun beating down on the steel roof, together with the heat of the laboring engine, makes the cab a furnace. I open the ventilators and get a blast of hot air in the face. Through the dark sunglasses my eyes slowly tick off the familiar landmarks: a clump of bushes, a sand dune, a native kraal. From these spots I can figure exactly when I'll be home.

We Order priests and brothers have our regular hours for formal prayer and meditation in the chapel, morning, noon, and evening. But our periods of meditation are not limited to the chapel. In that warm truck on the Mkuzi Run rolling and bumping over the dull bushveld much genuine and fruitful meditation is done: "Look at my soft skinny hands gripping this big tough wheel, these short pants and dirty sweat shirt — surely not priestly garb; but clothes don't make the priest. How did the bosses ever get it into their revered heads to send me here? — the will of God. But I was a teacher, working close to a fat and fancy degree when I got the African order, and physically I'm far from Atlas! — the Vow of Obedience." On and on your mind wanders with the constant drumming of the powerful engine. No, it's not precise and orderly, this type of meditation. But what religious can dance along the purgative road of Rodriguez while double-clutching in heavy sand!

Then there's the loneliness. Who likes to be alone? No one, missionaries included. But we are, again and again, for long stretches too, alone as only a white missionary can be in black Africa. We're alone in that hot, bouncing, creaking cab; and being alone we seek company, often His.

It's getting dark. I switch on the headlights and watch for the Star of the Sea bushes. When I begin to see this particular type of bush I know I'm about ten miles from home. The lorry boys too, riding up there on the load, keep a wary eye for the familiar landmarks; they are anxious to get the day's work done and sit around their fires with their wives and children. The more tired you are, the longer the landmarks take to appear. Seeing them makes me perk up. It's not second wind — that was gone long ago. It's the thought of being close to home, inside a house, out of this blazing truck and off this lonely and ever-foreign bushveld.

Around a dune, over a hill, and I can see the mission lights. The sight is a thrill. They too can see mine; I flash them so they know it's me. Reaching the stream which runs next to the mission, I slowly and carefully wade the heavy load through the shallow water, get set at the wheel for the roaring climb up the hill and the swing into the mission grounds.

The greeting is brief and casual, but warm: "Here's a beer — have any trouble? Did you remember the extra bag of salt, and the kerosene?" Then a nice refreshing shower followed by supper. One more Mkuzi Run is over.

14. Tribal Justice

THERE are times on the missions when the dull routine of the slow-moving life of the missionary is suddenly broken up — smashed to pieces in fact. Times when he stumbles into primitive native life and finds the contrast overpowering. This happened one day when I left the Ingwavuma mission in the jeep to pay a visit to the local chief; I had no business with him to discuss, just found myself with a free afternoon and thought I'd pop in on him. Not knowing it was the day he holds court, I suddenly found myself in the midst of primitive tribal justice.

It was almost like being suddenly absorbed into a spectacular Hollywood movie, the kind that overwhelms you and snaps you out of life for the two hours you sit there wide-eyed. There was no mammoth screen, no buttered popcorn. My seat was not a plush push-back, but a straw mat on a cow dung floor. I wasn't in the cavernous dark of a U. S. theater, but in the dirty dark of a dusty Zulu hut.

It all seemed so unreal. An hour before, I was in the post office collecting some packages from America, discussing with the postman the troubled European situation, jet planes, colored television. Now I was suddenly thrown back centuries, witnessing the administration of the tribal law of a primitive people. In South Africa some native tribal law is still intact; the government permits the chiefs limited jurisdiction over the people. They have their own police, their own courts, and their own punishments. Today it was all on display for me.

Chief Zombizwe is a heavy, well-built man of middle age. His name in Zulu literally means: "the one who shall be called." The other natives will never call him by that name: it's disrespectful to say the name of the chief, even when referring to him. They substitute other names, such as, the great son (of the former chief), or, uncle, the one on the hill (his hut is on a hill). The outstanding feature of him and his family is their unusual eyes; they are slanty, almost like the Chinese. The chief is a handsome, thin-lipped native with a beautiful set of strong, white, even teeth. Royalty oozes from him; he speaks with a confident, commanding air, sometimes fatherly, sometimes threateningly; his long thin hands are expressive, his many jestures are simple and graceful. Even his cross-legged posture on the mat next to me was distinguished and easy.

It wasn't my first visit — the relaxed atmosphere showed that. They were used to me. The chief seemed genuinely pleased to see a missionary with a young face and no long beard; and before inviting me into his hut he had pointed a curled forefinger at me (polite natives never point with a straight finger unless they want to insult you), and in soft Zulu said, "Your face, Umfundisi, will never carry much fur." Everybody laughed, and I didn't mind it. After that I asked him to continue his court cases and got his okay to sit in on them. For the next two hours the otherworldness of it all had me spellbound.

The hut was larger than most, but just as disorderly and dirty. There was a smouldering fire in the center to take the damp chill away. About seven or eight "bigs" of the tribe, all males, sat around the circular mud wall, their bare black legs pulled up, their animal skin loincloths pulled down, and their heads at a respectful tilt toward the chief. I assumed a similar position next to him. There was an unoccupied space in front of Zombizwe just inside the low-cut entrance. Here the accused and witnesses, prosecutor, and stray dogs took their places.

One man seemed to be running things, an old fellow with a peg leg, one eye, and memories of the Boer War. The chief whispered to him and he in turn whispered to others. There was always hushed talking among the men except when the chief decided to say something — anything. Then complete silence, followed by a chorus of low grunts of approval when he finished. It was hard to catch all their low Zulu, so I read faces and stumbled after the words. I caught pleased comments on the fact that a white man would now see their own customs of court. During the whole time I had said hardly a word.

The chief nodded for the first case and two men poked their heads into the low entrance from the bright outside. It was always dark inside, but we were blacked out completely when someone entered or left. They saluted the chief from their knees — clasped hands as in prayer, made a low bow, and a solemn and respectful pronouncement of one of the chief's respectful names. No one passed the entrance without going through that routine, and no one rushed it either; those darting, restless eyes of the chief missed nothing.

One of the men before him had accused the other of spoiling his daughter before he had given the full number of cattle required for her. The other didn't deny it, just calmly mentioned he was still trying to pay up for his first wife. A simple charge, but it was tucked away in twenty minutes of verbosity. The chief didn't mind the padding and never took his eyes off the men during the unwrapping.

During the ensuing silence I expected the chief to issue a punishment. Instead he nodded for the next case, then motioned the first two men to remain, but to move aside and make room for the others. The chief seemed full of grunts and nods whose meanings were understood immediately by the others. He seldom spoke out clearly while the evidence was being heard. This next case was that of a young man who had promised to put thatch on the roof of his uncle's hut for two pounds. He had taken the money and left the uncle roofless. Reason: he got drunk with the two pounds and was put in the white-man's jail for three months. When everything was heard, the uncle and nephew were likewise told to step aside and remain. Not the slightest hint of a decision was as yet given.

The third and fourth cases were much the same, squabbles over cattle for unpaid-for and un-intact daughters. The hut was becoming crowded and still the chief would not dismiss anyone and would not pass judgment. Instead, he shifted interest to his medicine man who was sitting next to me, on my left. He was a most interesting character, this man of medicine. Seemed oblivious of everything around him. Never lifted his bulging bloodshot eyes, seldom stirred, and assumed a superior air toward all but me. I suppose he considered the priest somewhere on a professional par!

He plied his trade well and seemed to revel in it. Around his neck hung a string of large teeth from various animals; across his chest was another string of small glass bottles each filled with a different colored powder. This is the distinctive livery of a medicine man. Pockets and pouches hung all over his chest and waist. During the two hours I watched him, he was busy with a sharp pocket knife whittling tiny pieces of wood and herbs into very fine particles. At intervals he would open a bottle on his neck, make a funny sign over it, wince his ugly face, and deposit the new mixture inside. All his ingredients he treated with reverent care and solemnity.

The medicine man merely diverted the chief's attention — he did not absorb it. While he was ostensibly watching the nimble hands, the chief often took long, penetrating looks at the four defendants and their accusers. Obviously he was trying to form his decision; yet he never said a word about the cases. He talked about the weather, his ailments, my presence among them, this year's crops — everything but what the hutful of men were waiting for, myself included. The others, too, came and joined in the small talk, somewhat listlessly however, since they were more concerned about the decisions.

Finally the chief motioned for silence. He then spoke four simple sentences, moving his head and eyes four times exactly:

"You are fined two cattle." "You are excused." "You give me two bulls and send the girl back." "You give me three cows." The words were clear and deliberate. No notes were taken, no records kept, not a word more was spoken by anyone. The four parties nodded full agreement, made humble bows, and left quietly. The chief snuffed himself heavily, flushed out a hidden flea, and called for the next case.

And so it went on for about two hours. It seemed unreal to me because it was so much different from my idea of a courtroom. There was no formality. Men sat in loincloths not wigs and gowns; there were no desks, no papers. Still there was an air of seriousness. To be fined two cattle is not a light matter. The expressions on the men's faces as they looked at the chief were not like men looking at a judge in a minor court in America. They were more like those of young seminarians looking at a Roman cardinal addressing them — respectful, admiring, reverent, and fearful. The fire and smoke and ashes in the center accentuated the primitiveness.

The chief finally became restless and said he would continue the cases in a few days. The litigants who remained would have to find shelter nearby and wait until the chief decided to open court again. I rose to my feet respectfully — I had been greatly impressed with the two hours. I complimented Chief Zombizwe on his swift and understanding administration of justice tempered with fatherliness; told him that we white people could take a lesson from some of his people's good customs; told him I would never forget this courtroom scene. And I haven't. Then I shook hands with him and the other men, stooped through the low entrance, and went out into the fresh air and bright sunlight. Walking over to the jeep was like walking away from a gripping play back to the parking lot. In the jeep I rubbed my eyes, stretched, and gradually came back to reality.

15. "All Things to All Men"

WHEN St. Paul uttered the wise advice to priests that they should be all things to all men we know he meant that priests should enter into all fields of human endeavor. He meant that we should have chameleon ability to adjust ourselves to any situation in order to further the cause of Christ, as he himself did. He no doubt would have intended that we missionaries should even become bush bogeymen, because, to many of these hinterland natives, that's just what we are.

Backward natives, the kind we are dealing with mostly, have little enough idea about white people in general: three meals a day, running water, so many clothes, flying through the air, talking boxes — all the whiteman customs and things amaze them. But a priest they can't figure out at all. He doesn't have a store, he doesn't have a jail, he doesn't even have *one* wife! He's nothing if not a great big bogeyman.

That last, having no wife, is a major hurdle for their simple minds to scale. It's a standard question while visiting kraals of a virgin area — how come celibacy? The first time a green missionary is peppered with it from several natives at once he comes out the loser, especially when he is short on Zulu. I had my initiation in a kraal of three wives, a man, and one smart young girl. The man and girl knew about Catholic priests being celibates; they had both worked in Johannesburg for some time. The less-traveled wives of the kraal knew nothing about us. To make conversation one of them inquired about the health

164

of my wife. (She thought I had left her overseas to take care of the house and kids.) It was easy to say I didn't have a wife, just two Zulu words: "Anginawo umfazi." The other two wives looked at me nonplused. I innocently asked, "Didn't you know that Roman priests do not take wives?" Their mouths dropped open. The man and girl could have helped me with a slight explanation, but they, enjoying my discomfort, merely looked demurely at the floor waiting for me to stumble on. I glanced back at the wives and caught them eyeing me up and down, curiously and thoroughly.

"No, we Catholic priests don't take wives, none of us," I repeated weakly. The second wife said, "But you have a nice house, a car, a horse; surely you can afford to buy yourself a wife — even two!" I understood her Zulu okay, and gulped. The other wife added wide-eyed, "And here you are a fully grown man!" Natives call a spade a spade. I gulped again. Why the blazes didn't the seminary teach us how to respond to Zulu wives!

The stock answers bubbled to mind, but in my chopped-up Zulu they fell flat. Even the most eloquent Zulu could not communicate the idea of voluntary celibacy to this audience. This family listened attentively to my sputtering: the sharp girl sported a knowing smile and nodded a grand unbelieving yes to each of my sentences. The man quickly agreed with every word, looking on me as a young, pleasant, polite liar. These two did know about priests being celibates, but they really didn't believe it. They were enjoying my fumbling answers, half from their fun-loving nature, and half from a now-we-got-him attitude. The poor wives were totally dumb-struck, nothing moved on their faces except their lips and eyelids, which drew farther apart at each sentence. A week later I passed them on a path and they looked at me in the same curious way!

Other times the priest's being white strikes the native with genuine fear. Walking up to a kraal one day, I approached a small group of people sitting in the shade of a tree. "Look at the white man — don't be afraid," the mother softly urged the squirming child in her arms. There was a quiet moment as the baby slowly turned to me, eyes bulging. They focused on my face, popped more as the impression went home, then out came a fierce yowl. It was her first look at a white man. The mother coddled her and laughingly assured I wouldn't hurt. But it didn't work. She buried her tiny shaking frame in the mother's bosom and would not dare look up. The hysteria spread to the other children, who dropped the grasshoppers they had been playing with and scampered into the hut, wailing.

The bedlam was not serious and was nothing new. Fear of sheltered natives at the first sight of a white priest is a daily affair. The secret is to be patient and extremely relaxed. Your calmness is contagious. Smiling to me pleasantly the mother explained how the children had never been to the store to see the white man there. She could see I was used to the situation and was not perturbed. Inside the hut the three kids had stopped crying and were peeking at me through the reed walls. I quietly told them not to be scared but to come out and let me see their pretty faces. One ventured her head out the entrance. Soothingly, the mother told her to take the good mat down from the wall and bring it out for me. She hesitated, looked me over again while I stood motionless, then got the mat and laid it next to me, conquered.

Helping the children and some adults over that white skin fear is only the first hurdle in effective visiting. There is an enormous amount of thornier underbrush that must be cleared from their bogeyman. Occasionally we come across a thinking native who has already prepared the ground for you. Natives believe in God and understand their duty of homage to Him. Some go further and catch on that you, white or black, wifeless or not, are a means of rendering God that homage.

There's an old man in this Ingwavuma area whom it's a genuine pleasure to visit. He's an oasis in this desert of ignorance, superstition, and misunderstanding. He is always happy to see me stroll up his path. He gets out a block to sit on, tells his wives and children to gather around, and makes no false fuss. He seems to be continually studying me with his beady observant eyes, never missing a movement I make, catching every voice inflection, every flick of my eyes. And he does this naturally, without offense. His keen mind never stops registering.

No, he doesn't come to church, nor do his wives. But recently he told me he was thinking of chancing one of his girls in our school providing we don't make a nun of her and deprive him of fifteen head of cattle from her suitor. He doesn't talk about religion often, but after a long silence between us — and long silences are a vital part of native conversation — he'll come out with a sincere question. A question indicating some wheels had been turning. "Umfundisi, why don't *all* the white people go to church since they know so much about everything?" Umfundisi, what is your country like? Do you have any sisters or brothers?" "Umfundisi, why did you become an Umfundisi?" It's only a short step from the subject of the Umfundisi to that of his Church.

Some of the natives never lick their bogeyman fear of us. With them, repeated friendly visits over a period of years fail to span the white-black gap. I had been in charge of the main mission at Ingwavuma for over four years, I had come to know the people well, could fluently speak their language, but still I often found myself reaching after them desperately and unsuccessfully. There was a woman at the foot of our Ingwavuma mountain whom I often visited yet never saw except at a great distance through a pair of binoculars. Halfway down the mountain I usually get off the horse and give us both a breather, "Take ten," I tell him with a pat on his long nose. It's pleasant to look out over the vast low veld and pick out the tiny huts far below — the binoculars draw them right up to you. The people can be seen moving around their huts. One kraal was set apart from the others, perhaps a few city blocks.

From my mountain perch I often saw a woman working near this lonely hut.

The people below can see me coming; my white coat reflects the sun, and it takes about an hour to climb down. Everything is fine until I reach this particular kraal. The little hut door is always closed and tied with grass rope. This is not unusual in itself — it's a sign no one is home. But glancing around the yard I see a freshly burning fire, some half-peeled potatoes and the inevitable black three-legged iron cooking pot with the water hot. Obviously someone just left the place in a hurry. I tie up the horse and wait ten minutes. Most people get back in that time. No one comes. The stillness is broken only by chickens clucking and by the usual forest noises from the surrounding bush.

And in that bush is where the woman is; she runs there every time I come. There's no way to get her out, and I don't dare go in after her. I call out, "Hello, is anyone here! I'm a priest not the police. I want to talk to you about coming to the Roman Church!" I'm sure she hears me from her hiding place, but she gives no sign. I have told the people around her to let her know I'd like to talk to her and that I'm quite harmless. They too get a laugh out of her fears. I hear from them how deathly afraid she is of white skin, and that she never goes near the village. It's a senseless fear, but there's no denying it — the people often seem like children with their suspicions and fears — she was like a kid afraid of the dark, and there was no getting around it by force. She would even like to go to church, but she is afraid. With a telling gesture they also assure me that there is nothing wrong with her mind.

They promised me that they would explain well to her about me and that the next time I come I would see her. A month later I spotted her with the glasses again, and went down the mountain; but she had again disappeared. So it was until the last time I went there. Then things were different. The hut door was wide open, and there was no fire. There was nothing fresh about the place except her nearby grave. She had died of malaria, while I was still a bogeyman to her.

The missionary priest is also a constant "soapboxer." A native man once asked me: "Say, Umfundisi, where is the country you come from?" We were sitting around his yard with his wives and children. He had no idea of geography, no idea of the number of countries besides his own. His was not the first native question I ever fumbled. I went after it from five different angles, my Zulu growing worse as their minds fogged with ideas of distance and nations. As I beat the air relentlessly, the wives started side conversations, the kids played with stones. The old guy's expression went from utter confusion to one of disappointment. Another question the white man can't answer, where his own country is!

With that I made use of my handy riding crop. With it I marked an x in the dirt at my feet and told them that it was their country. Then I made a long line to another x, explaining there was water between and the months and months it would take to travel the distance. The second x was England, a place they had heard of because of the Boer War. The wives stopped talking and the kids stopped playing when they saw me draw another long line leading to another x, "And this is my country, America," I said. The old man beamed with pleasure. The children laughed and the wives nodded. Light had struck.

And I said to myself: here I am again on the old soapbox. Again and always. After a few years in Africa the missionary realizes his perch is just that. Instructing, explaining, exhorting, correcting, showing. Not necessarily religious topics either; everything under the sun — with the exception of politics, which we avoid. The natives look to us for their slightest wants, come to us with their most serious problems. Paternalism is in their very veins, and priests answer to Father.

There's no such thing as missionary office hours, professional time. It's a full time, delightful, mountain-moving job. You can't step off that soapbox for long — our good Zulus won't let you. White skin is blue blood in South Africa; yet the royalty of a missionary is not beyond reach. . . . He's kind, affable, our missionary priest, let's ask him about everything. He doesn't make fun of our questions, he doesn't condemn us continually. He sometimes even appreciates us. . . . And so they come to us, and by means of our perennial soapboxing we try to bridge the yawning chasm between white and black.

Two or three times a week some old Zulu comes in with: "Umfundisi, will you take me out across the mountain so I can visit my relative?" Often we do use our pickup for hauling natives twenty or thirty miles, but only for a good reason. Others see this and figure they'll cash in for any reason. You just can't say no and go back to your room. You must climb up on the ever-ready soapbox and explain how you would be very happy to help him if the relative were seriously sick, or you would take him along if you were going that way. But a special trip just to visit — impossible.

Incomprehension stands out in his black eyes. There's the truck, drums of gas in the yard, and he saw the other natives riding often on the priest's pickup. So you explain that those things are not ours to use as we please. They are the Church's; they were bought with money from Catholics across the waters. The Catholics, many of them poorer than you, gave that money to help spread the Church. I can't misuse the truck and gas by taking natives around the country just for visits. That's not spreading the Church. He seems to catch on. He humbly bows, says he now understands clearly, and leaves pleasantly. You take a breath, step down — but leave the soapbox in a handy place.

With sickness and wounds you have a natural set-up for your teaching. You find a man lying in a hut with a festering sore on his foot, gangrenous and blown up. He won't go to the hospital — that's a place to die. So you wash and bandage the foot, and perhaps give him some pills. He's hesitant; can't see how little gray pills are going to get down to his foot. You tell him they'll make his blood strong, and that does go down to his foot; in fact it's oozing out of his foot right now, dark and smelly. If you please you may go on, telling him how you too take these same pills for infections. Our blood is the same really. His eyes widen. Yes, you insist, same qualities in both. Like our souls. There are not two heavens and two hells, not one for black people and one for white people . . . On and on, establishing closer contact, germinating the seeds of understanding, preparing the ground for faith.

You can laugh at their questions, even openly; they love it — as long as your laugh has no ridicule in it. At the end of my Monday morning catechism class with the school children I have a question period. While we were discussing the story of Adam and Eve, one morning a little guy upped with: "Umfundisi, what was the surname of Adam and Eve?" Surnames are important to Zulus. There was silence — they wanted to know. I shattered it with, "Gumede," which is a common local surname. It brought the house down — best laugh I ever got.

This soapboxing is more effective when done gently, even with the most obvious mistakes. When I leave an outstation to come back to Ingwavuma there are usually five or six people around asking for a ride; old women going to collect their pension, men going to pay their tax, maybe some kids for shopping. I tell them to hop on, and the men and kids do just that, leaving the old women to struggle for themselves over the tail gate of the pickup. A sight like that tempts me to blast them hard, the thoughtless men and kids. But I rein myself in. Natives can't understand anger in their priests. However, I don't give them a pious recitation of "She's somebody's mother, boys, you know," but I tell them in no uncertain terms to get off and help the old women on and give them the best places in the truck. Next month, next year, the same things may happen with the same set of people. You get back up there on the box and go at it again.

Slowly, ever so slowly, this continuous, persevering, fatherliness rubs off on them. And in its wake are the wonders of baptism, Christian Life, eternity in heaven. Our good, wholesome, lovable Zulu people, God-loving, God-fearing, the numberless thirsty thousands of them, parched by paganism, are aching for the waters of Apollo.

After almost seven years from the day I first landed in Johannesburg word came from our Provincial Office in Chicago that it was now my turn to go home on a six-month furlough. My hands shook with excitement as I read the letter. Father Kucera, who was assigned to take my place at Ingwavuma, would be coming from Good Shepherd Mission in a few days. All I had to do was show him the outstation schedule and arrange my passage home. Inside I was jumping.

The day before I left Ingwavuma for Johannesburg the school children put on a show for me. Parents, teachers, sisters, catechists, priests, and brothers were there huddled in our large classroom; the whole parish had been invited through Mass announcements the previous Sunday. The kids went all out — songs, dances, skits. They had become close to me and were anxious to display their affection now that I was leaving. It wouldn't do for me to make a sentimental fool of myself before everyone, but it took all I had not to. The little lad who years ago imitated my preaching for Father General's show was now a fully grown teenager, one of our altar boys. He recited a home-made Zulu poem that he and the children and the teachers had composed. It thanked me warmly for all the instruction and correction I had given them, asked me never to tire helping the black people of Africa. There was also something in the poem about how they hoped I would find my parents and relatives well at home, but that they should not persuade me to stay there — the black people loved me, too, and needed me more. My eyes went down and I felt a twitch in my lips.

Others were there also: the old ex-army native who had given me a chicken on my first visit to his kraal; two of his wives

("C'mon you bloody fools"), one of them now a Catholic; the
"wise guy" whose father I had bandaged and who had become
a sensible married man now and sometimes came to Mass; the
two little brash dancing girls who shocked me at the tent, now
dressed in modest school uniforms, their First Communion already made. I found myself looking them all over, my mind
reeling. They too, as the show progressed were stealing long
looks at me. I called out between acts that they should not
drink too much beer while I was away, and be sure their
babies didn't cry in church during the new priest's sermons. Anything I said to them or they to me got laughs that afternoon.
Laughs cover a lot.

Arrived at the sprawling Johannesburg airport, I saw that it,
too, had changed since that first landing when I had stared wide-
eyed at the black laborers. Instead of the barren shacks of the
old Palmeitfontein airport there was a beautiful massive terminal
building at the new Jan Smuts airport. The weighing attendant
tied a tag on my beat-up traveling bag. The heavy black crayon
writing said "Midway Airport, Chicago, U. S. A." I fondled the
tag a moment as the man smiled knowingly. "Have a good trip,
Father!" he said.

Walking out to the ramp across the bright sunny expanse of
cement I passed a group of native workers coming from my
KLM Constellation. They were laughing loudly together. In
confident Zulu I cracked to them: "Sure you fellas put enough
fuel in that thing? I'm going a long way." Wide, white grins
came back, happy to have the priest kid with them in their own
tongue. "Yebo, that fat old girl has plenty in her belly. Go
well, Umfundisi!"

The roaring monster lifted off the long runway, climbed,
banked, and headed directly north. Sitting alone, I unfastened
the seat belt and let a thousand thoughts clamber in. The last
thing I had told the kids and adults at the show was to pray,
pray hard that I would be allowed to return. I wondered if their
prayers would be answered my way. . . . They were.